BLOK/EKO

Howard Barker

BLOK/EKO

OBERON BOOKS
LONDON

WWW.OBERONBOOKS.COM

First published in 2011 by Oberon Books Ltd
521 Caledonian Road, London N7 9RH
Tel: +44 (0) 20 7607 3637 / Fax: +44 (0) 20 7607 3629
e-mail: info@oberonbooks.com
www.oberonbooks.com

A catalogue record for this book is available from the British
Library.

ISBN: 978-1-84943-110-1

Cover image by Eduardo Houth

Printed in Great Britain by CPI Antony Rowe, Chippenham.

Characters

EKO	A Despot
QUOTA	Her Interpreter
NAUSICAA	Homer's Perfect Child in Later Life
TOT	A Poet
PINDAR	A Poet
BLOK	A Servant, Formerly a Poet
QUASIDOC	A Female Doctor
AUTHENTICUT	A Male Doctor
LAMP	One of a Crowd
SHEET	" " " "
RUBBER	" " " "
TRUCK	A Male Doctor
PALLID	A Female Doctor
BRADY	A Hirer of Guns
THE PUBLIC	
THE POLICE	

1

A vast floor, empty. The sound of a winch.

2

Rising through the floor, a seated woman, aged and naked. On arrival, she stares. She fathoms.

3

The slow beat of a pendulum.

4

The sound of a winch.

5

A slatted crate containing the bodies of two surgeons descends. The limbs of the surgeons protrude through the slats. The descent of the crate is infinitely slow.

6

A youth is discovered on the perimeter of the stage. He is motionless, his hands thrust in his pockets, his hat over his eyes.

7

A second woman enters, smartly dressed in hat and suit. She carries a tray with a single glass. She marches towards the old woman. She falls. The tray slides over the floor. The glass shatters. She lies without moving.

8

The winch. The pendulum.

9

As if in response to the sound of breaking glass, an old man inches on stage with a broom. In contrast to the fallen woman, his movements are stiff.

10

The old woman peers about. The crate descends. The old man arrives at the site of the accident, and sweeps. The sound of glass shards shifted.

11

Fragments. The winch. The pendulum.

12

As if she had never fallen at all, the second woman picks herself up.

NAUSICAA: The first three lines she likes / the first three / yes to those / she says / yes to the first three / much less liking for the rest /

(The old man inches out, having made a small heap of the fragments.)

The rest in / in / in /

(She agonizes with an impediment. The youth watches with indifference.)

Inchoate / she says /

TOT: Inchoate? /

NAUSICAA: Inchoate /

TOT: *(Contemptuous.)* Inchoate? /

NAUSICAA: *(Irritably.)* IN / IN / INCHOATE / SHE SAYS /

(The old man reappears with a dustpan.)

THE REST / so whilst / her confidence in you is un / un /

(She tosses her head in her agony.)

Undiminished / go back to it / she says /

(The old man stoops and sweeps the broken glass into the dustpan.)

The theme is good / in / in /

(Again she masters her speech.)

Intensify it / intensify the theme / she says /

13

A third woman, dressed identically to NAUSICAA, enters with the identical tray and glass. She walks in a more measured way to the old woman and stands behind her. The old man, painfully upright again, proceeds to leave. The crate of dead surgeons continues in its scarcely-perceptible descent. The youth is immobile, if incandescent.

14

The old woman sings in a cracked voice.

EKO: Examine me / oh my beloved surgeon / let your cold
hands run free / and your hot eyes / loosen them / like
dogs in meadows / give them their liberty / my breasts
reach for the grave / my thighs / like quicksands are my
thighs / tread carefully / or you will drown in me / my
lover / how shyly you avert your gaze / shyly / shyly /
who would know your secret / only me / only me /

*(She ceases. She is suffused by melancholy. No one has moved. Even
the old man, who has stopped for the duration of the song, hesitates
to continue. The descent of the dead surgeons completed, the crate
sways slightly, as if in a breeze. With a swift move EKO snatches
the glass off the tray and swallows the contents in one go. As if this
were a signal, the old man proceeds to leave. NAUSICAA, similarly
unlocked, sets out to leave. After a few paces, she falls as before. She
lies perfectly prostrate. The youth, ignoring NAUSICAA, launches
himself off the wall and goes to the old woman.)*

TOT: Exquisite / exquisite / not the song / the singing / the
singing of the song / your voice / if it is a voice / if that
parched / cracked / busted and encrusted / thing / is voice
at all / was / oh / who cares what name we give to it / was
more perfect than twelve boys / six eunuchs / anything /
you think I flatter / you think I ingratiate myself with you
/ sometimes I do / not today / not today I promise you /
when you sing now / it is /

(He creates a gesture.)

I don't know / it is /

*(His elaborations are curtailed by the second woman letting fall the
tray. It clatters to the floor. The glass shatters.)*

QUOTA: She cannot stomach your insincerity / or to be precise
/ she is offended by the exaggeration of whatever was
sincere /

TOT: Much was sincere /

QUOTA: In what you said /

TOT: Much / much / was sincere / if not everything / I promise you / but I /

(The old man inches on stage with the broom, as before.)

I acknowledge / exaggeration is a tendency to which I am / occasionally /

QUOTA: *(Cutting him off.)* She says undress me /

TOT: Occasionally / susceptible /

QUOTA: Now / she says / undress me now /

(The old man attends to the broken glass.)

TOT: In mitigation of this offence / it must be said /

QUOTA: NOW / NOW / SHE IS IMPATIENT /

(The broom. The sound of glass shards. The old man, having heaped the detritus, inches off-stage. As he goes, NAUSICAA swiftly rises to her feet and marches off in the opposite direction. TOT, with a certain reluctance, goes to QUOTA, who poses for his attention. TOT proceeds to unbutton her severe black costume.)

TOT: It must be said / in my own defence / that there is some inconsistency / is there not / in indicting me with exaggeration when / as everybody knows /

QUOTA: *(Severely.)* Don't say what everybody knows / do you know everybody? /

TOT: *(Ceasing unbuttoning, allowing his hands to fall to his sides.)* I don't know everybody / no /

QUOTA: UNDRESS ME / UNDRESS ME / SHE SAYS /

TOT: *(Returning to the buttons.)* Obviously I don't know what everybody knows / it was a / a /

QUOTA: *(Reprimanding TOT.)* Lazy /

TOT: A figure of speech /

QUOTA: Lazy she says /

TOT: Yes / it is lazy to employ figures of speech /

QUOTA: Especially in poets /

TOT: *(Humiliated.)* In poets especially / yes /

(The old man reappears with the dustpan and brush. He inches towards the heaped glass. TOT does not pursue his defence. Having unbuttoned QUOTA to the waist he draws back the upper half of her clothing, exposing her breasts. There is a brief suggestion of reluctance in TOT's manner, immediately detected.)

QUOTA: Are you interested / she says / are you really interested? /

TOT: *(Trapped.)* Interested? / am I / am I /

QUOTA: INTERESTED / ARE YOU / YES / SHE SEES NO POINT IN PURSUING A THING FOR WHICH YOU SEEM TO LACK THE APPETITE /

(The old man kneels, sweeps.)

She cares for you / and wishes you to know this caring / not only to know / to experience it /

TOT: I am aware of this caring /

QUOTA: Are you? / Good /

TOT: Aware and profoundly grateful /

QUOTA: Excellent / she says / but /

TOT: *(Predicting QUOTA's admonition.)* AND IN STATING THIS I DO NOT EXAGGERATE /

(The sound of the broom, the glass. The old man staggers to his feet. He moves painfully away.)

QUOTA: Proceed then / proceed to undress me /

(TOT seems to recover confidence. He takes time to observe QUOTA's nakedness, his hands moving in his tension. Now he tears more vigorously at the remainder of the costume. QUOTA is still as a mannequin. EKO senses all and observes nothing. TOT kisses QUOTA, who remains unmoved but compliant. They stagger. EKO sings.)

15

EKO: His lips were strong / stronger than an army / they burned / they stripped / they devoured me /

(The old man passes and ignores the entrance of a bound doctor, propelled by two men who manhandle him into the vast room. The doctor struggles, but is gagged and soundless. The peculiar ballet of their progress distracts neither TOT nor EKO.)

My husband stopped me on the stairs / what are you hiding there / behind your hand / my devious and lying love? /

(The doctor is forced down and fixed to the floor.)

A swollen lip / oh / what stung you / a hornet / or a honey bee? /

(QUOTA is taken by TOT and forcing a hand in her mouth, attempts to stifle her cry. It nevertheless erupts and punctuates EKO's song.)

I was stung / oh so badly stung / while eating fruit / I feel the poison spread through me /

(QUOTA is still. TOT also. Their perfection achieved. In the silence, EKO's small, sweet old woman's laugh. Now QUOTA separates herself from TOT and adjusts her clothing, walking in a small circle as she does up each of the many buttons to the neck.)

16

A desperate cry from offstage announces the appearance of a second knot of struggling men, hauling a woman in a white coat.

QUASIDOC: NOT A DOCTOR / NOT A DOCTOR / NOT A DOCTOR ME /

(The prisoner is hauled into the room. TOT, emboldened by his success with the still-revolving QUOTA, advances to within touching distance of EKO, whose gaze remains fixed on the horizon.)

TOT: When you say inchoate / I have to say this /

QUASIDOC: NOT A DOCTOR I SAID /

TOT: You are employing a critical vocabulary which / whilst not redundant / cannot be / like some spanner fixed to a leaking tap / simply clamped to my imagination and tightened / my poetry /

QUASIDOC: THEY PUT THIS COAT ON ME /

(The men constraining QUASIDOC stifle her.)

TOT: Obeys its own laws / one of which insists upon a certain /

QUOTA: *(Still buttoning.)* She knows this /

TOT: A certain familiarity with common speech /

QUOTA: She knows this perfectly well /

TOT: Common speech which / by definition / is unrefined /

QUOTA: She knows everything you are saying /

TOT: Of course she does /

(He persists nevertheless.)

Therefore / what might seem inchoate is / in fact / as finished as it can be / and relies / for its effect / entirely / on this somewhat / I admit / superficially / coarse character /

QUOTA: She knows /

TOT: ALL RIGHT / SHE KNOWS /

(His outburst is regretted at once. He moves his fingers uncomfortably.)

Ask her / please / ask her if she thinks by removing all that is / is /

(He squirms.)

INCHOATE / in my poem / I might be considered for a prize /

(He stares at the floor.)

I need the money /

QUOTA: She knows this also /

TOT: *(Resigned.)* Does she? /

QUOTA: She knows how badly you need the money /

(TOT abandons his cause. He turns to go.)

Rob a shop / she says / a handbag / snatch one /

(TOT looks resentfully at the back of EKO. QUOTA, her clothing restored, brushes the dress swiftly with one hand. TOT, decayed by failure, goes to leave.)

Her confidence is undiminished /

(TOT looks up grimly.)

Her confidence / and admiration / undiminished / she says /

(He goes to leave.)

And wait /

(TOT stops.)

She cares for you /

(TOT, in his bewilderment, strokes his face, and goes to leave again.)

And wait /

(He is obedient.)

Greater than her love of you / is her love of poetry /

(He seems to boil in his frustration, and again goes to leave.)

Wait / she says /

(He suffers, and stops.)

Few ever had / or ever will / possess your talent /

(TOT stares at the back of EKO, still as sculpture.)

TOT: FUCK THAT / I SAY / FUCK THAT / FUCK HER / FUCK YOU /

(EKO's eerie laugh comes from her stillness. TOT marches out. QUASIDOC escapes the grip of her oppressors.)

QUASIDOC: IT DOESN'T FIT / THE COAT / IT DOESN'T FIT / IF I WAS A DOCTOR /

(They try to silence her.)

I'D HAVE A COAT THAT FITTED / WOULDN'T I? / A COAT THAT FITTED PROPERLY? / OR IS THAT /

(They press on her. QUOTA leaves smartly.)

Is that / is that /

(They force her to the floor.)

Is that / is that / too logical for you?

17

A second crate is discovered, descending. This, like the first, contains executed doctors, whose limbs protrude through the slats.

18

NAUSICAA enters with her characteristic energy, a voluminous garment of wool, half-coat, half-blanket, extended before her with both hands.

NAUSICAA: She's naked / I said / naked / he said / nothing could be more in / in / in /

(She drapes EKO with the garment and proceeds to enclose her.)

Intriguing / in / in / inspiring and / in / in / he does this deliberately / inflammable / to me / inflammable / I said / that's inaccurate / surely / can one say / of a human being / that he / or she / is inflammable? / What you mean to say is this / the sight of her naked / might in / in / inflame me / that makes me inflammable / he said / I disagree /

QUASIDOC: *(Escaping briefly but seized again.)* I'm not a doctor / please / please / I never was a doctor / ever / never / ever / was I a doctor / not a student / not a nurse / nothing/ not even / a /

(They grapple her.)

a /

a /

(She is silenced. Her horrified gaze meets the gaze of the first victim, fixed to the floor by his guards in an identical way.)

19

A young man, of exquisite appearance, enters. His gaze falls on the trapped doctors and on the still-descending second crate. QUOTA enters briskly, carrying a glass on a tray.)

QUOTA: She loves the poem / loves it /

PINDAR: Thank you /

QUOTA: An exquisite thing / she says /

PINDAR: Thank you /

QUOTA: *(Posting herself alongside EKO.)* Whilst possibly the most accomplished refinement of your style it nevertheless suggests / without the least contrivance / stylistic and thematic innovations she expects will emerge in greater definition later / like all your poetry / she says / she chooses her words carefully / it succeeds in being both dazzling and effortless /

(PINDAR tilts in acknowledgement.)

Dazzling and effortless /

(EKO snatches the glass off the tray, swallows the contents and replaces it.)

PINDAR: These compliments /

QUOTA: Not compliments /

(PINDAR is rebuked, and hesitates before resuming his theme.)

PINDAR: These perceptive remarks /

(He is not interrupted, so he proceeds.)

These perceptive remarks / I need hardly say /

NAUSICAA: Say anyway /

(PINDAR looks to NAUSICAA.)

Say anyway / she says /

PINDAR: I will say / are of such significance to me / I no longer experience them as pleasure / but rather / and I am the first to recognize how this places me in jeopardy / as the necessary basis of my moral and physical existence / lending me the confidence / not only to thrash my imagination to yet further exertions / but also to ask things artists of lesser authority might hesitate to do /

(He raises his chin.)

For example /

(He affects a nonchalance.)

The extermination of the doctors /

(QUOTA lets fall the tray, with the usual shattering effect. PINDAR proceeds as if he sensed the inevitability of this reaction.)

An admirable initiative but now / I think / carried
to excess / the zeal with which these individuals are
apprehended / and the sheer number of them / causing me
/ and not only me / to suspect /

(The old man inches on with a broom.)

Innocent bystanders are /

QUASIDOC: *(Who has followed this.)* LIKE ME / LIKE ME /

PINDAR: Being swept up in some /

QUASIDOC: LIKE ME /

QUOTA: Careful / she says /

NAUSICAA: Careful /

PINDAR: Careful / yes / some torrent of undiscriminating
persecution which /

NAUSICAA/QUOTA: CAREFUL / SHE SAYS /

(PINDAR hesitates, the vehemence of the women intimidating him. He places his hands together, a plea and a calculated gesture of sensibility.)

PINDAR: If /

If /

If /

(He walks a few paces, calculating.)

If I am great /

(The old man, arriving, sweeps glass.)

And the award of so many prizes inclines me to think so /

(He poses.)

IF I AM /

(The sound of the broom. QUASIDOC stares.)

Let the state that honours me /

NAUSICAA/QUOTA: VERY / VERY /

PINDAR: Yes /

NAUSICAA/QUOTA: CAREFUL NOW /

PINDAR: *(Appearing to heed them.)* Yes / yes /

(He fills his lungs. the broom sweeps.)

SHOW THE SAME GENEROSITY TO THOSE / NOT EVEN
DOCTORS /

QUASIDOC: LIKE ME /

PINDAR: CAUGHT UP IN A RAGE / AN UNDISCRIMINATING
RAGE /

QUASIDOC: LIKE ME /

PINDAR: The real doctors are all dead / surely? /

20

*A stillness. The old man inches out on squeaking soles. PINDAR's fists
open and close in his excitement.*

NAUSICAA: *(At last.)* Firstly /

(She appears to listen.)

Firstly / she says /

PINDAR: *(In a reckless initiative.)* What a beautiful / oh what a / what a / what a very beautiful / gown is it? / Coat? / Gown? / Gown surely? / I did not take it in / the beauty of the gown / I was blinded by vanity / thinking / as always / always the thought obsessing me / does she like the poem? / When all the time / a greater poem / yes / a poem of grey wool / if it is wool / yes / wool surely? / Should have distracted me / is it wool? / The poem she is wearing? /

(NAUSICAA allows PINDAR to finish before resuming.)

NAUSICAA: Firstly / she emphasizes / with a certain in / in / indignation / that no prize awarded here is awarded out of generosity /

PINDAR: No /

NAUSICAA: And discrimination /

PINDAR: Yes /

NAUSICAA: Discrimination alone justifies the giving of the prize /

PINDAR: Of course /

NAUSICAA: Would you have it any other way? /

PINDAR: No / I would not / no /

NAUSICAA: She goes on /

PINDAR: Yes /

NAUSICAA: To say /

PINDAR: Yes /

(NAUSICAA strains to transmit the message.)

NAUSICAA: To say / to remind / to remind you / that your ability to manufacture sonnets / in no way /

PINDAR: Manufacture? /

NAUSICAA: In no way qualifies you /

PINDAR: Manufacture / did she say? /

QUOTA: *(Rebuking PINDAR.)* Shh /

NAUSICAA: To issue judgements of a political / or social / nature /

PINDAR: *(Lowering his head.)* Thank her for this timely reminder of the limitations of /

QUOTA: Shh /

PINDAR: My talent /

NAUSICAA: However /

PINDAR: *(Gnawing.)* But did she say /

QUOTA: SHH /

NAUSICAA: She goes on / if you prefer it / you may have the doctor who claims to be no doctor / as a substitute for what / she senses / is the somewhat tarnished / and routine award of yet another /

QUASIDOC: THAT'S ME /

PINDAR: *(Horrified.)* Tarnished? / Did I ever say /

QUASIDOC: ME / ME /

NAUSICAA: Another prize /

PINDAR: NEVER / NEVER HAVE I INDICATED THE SLIGHTEST INGRATITUDE FOR / OR / COMPLACENCY WITH REGARD TO / OR / OR /

(He shudders with frustration. The old man inches on stage with the dustpan and broom.)

I LOVE ALL PRIZES / OH / BELIEVE ME WHEN I SAY I LOVE THE PRIZE /

(He stares at NAUSICAA, then at QUOTA, but nothing comes from EKO now.)

21

The squeaking soles of the old man. PINDAR seems to suffer a collapse, his hands hang in his ordeal.

QUASIDOC: THAT'S ME /

(The old man arrives.)

OH / LET ME BE YOUR PRIZE / LET ME / I'VE TWO SO-LOVELY CHILDREN / OH SO-LOVELY /

(The broom sweeps. the glass tinkles. at last PINDAR makes a gesture, half-reluctant, towards QUASIDOC, who, registering it, hangs her head.)

Thank you /

(The old man sets off.)

Thank you /

(Without a signal, EKO descends, slowly, impassively. PINDAR longs to, but cannot discover the appropriate speech. His body evinces this. QUOTA marches swiftly offstage. The men constraining QUASIDOC free her, throwing her down. They drift away. The second doctor, seizing the moment, rips the gag from his mouth.)

AUTHENTICUT: SHE IS A DOCTOR / AND SHE'S GOT NO KIDS /

(His brief cry is subdued. He is rushed off by his captors, his feet dragging on the floor.)

22

PINDAR is suffused by wretchedness. NAUSICAA regards him with contempt. QUASIDOC crouches, as if to make herself invisible.

NAUSICAA: *(Biting her lip.)* Fraud /

PINDAR: Not in front of /

NAUSICAA: FRAUD / I SAID /

PINDAR: *(Brutally.)* NOT IN FRONT OF A /

(He looks at QUASIDOC. He cannot help himself delivering a spiteful kick to the doctor.)

NAUSICAA: It is so terrible to love a fraud / so in / in / in /

(This time NAUSICAA does not seek to complete the word, though her head twists on her neck.)

I have a weakness / an in / in / incurable weakness for /

(She aches.)

Liars and frauds /

PINDAR: She is manipulative / so very / very manipulative /

NAUSICAA: And you are fraudulent / so very / very fraudulent /

PINDAR: *(Ignoring her.)* Sometimes / it's obvious to me / she is scarcely aware how manipulative she is /

NAUSICAA: Whereas you / you are / you are aware how fraudulent you are /

PINDAR: It's a way of life to her /

NAUSICAA: Ha /

PINDAR: And like all mischief which is permitted to become a way of life /

NAUSICAA: Ha /

PINDAR: It breeds its own dilemmas /

NAUSICAA: HA /

PINDAR: *(Gravely.)* Nausicaa / you know I refrain from striking women /

NAUSICAA: HA /

PINDAR: And knowing this / you take advantage of the fact / may I / therefore / urge you to imagine I have slapped your face /

NAUSICAA: *(Immediately imagining it.)* OW /

PINDAR: Suffer the indignation that would certainly have accompanied that slap /

NAUSICAA: OW /

PINDAR: AND PERMIT ME TO FINISH WHAT I AM / IN MY CRISIS / TRYING TO ARTICULATE AND SHARE WITH YOU /

(He froths.)

NAUSICAA /

(She glares at PINDAR.)

NAUSICAA: You are a fraud / oh God / in all you say and do / a fraud / Pindar /

(He glares at her in turn.)

PINDAR: Who will get the prize if I don't? / Who? / There's no one / Tot? / Ha / Tot? / Now I'm laughing / TOT / TOT / I'm more than laughing / I'm hysterical / no / she has / as I was explaining / in her relentless mischief / created a dilemma /

(He frowns, winces.)

THE PRIZE ITSELF IS MOCKED / THE PRIZE ITSELF IS SPOILED / RIDICULED / DIMINISHED /

NAUSICAA: Undress for me /

PINDAR: WHAT PRIZE? YOU'D WANT TO WASH YOUR HANDS AFTER ACCEPTING IT /

(NAUSICAA gazes on PINDAR. She goes towards him, and is about to place a hand on him when QUASIDOC speaks.)

QUASIDOC: I'm the prize /

(NAUSICAA goes to loosen PINDAR's garment with a single outstretched hand.)

ME /

(PINDAR hears and heeds the kneeling doctor. Ignoring NAUSICAA, he swiftly turns.)

PINDAR: A PRIZE SPEAKS /

(He laughs, with the delight of discovery.)

ON YOUR FEET / PRIZE / AND FOLLOW ME /

(The doctor scrambles up, similarly radiant. PINDAR's brow is darkened by the offence offered to NAUSICAA.)

Odysseus / who took your filthy innocence / wished to die beside his wife / the warrior lacked the courage for the new life Nausicaa in / in /

(PINDAR enjoys his parody.)

Invited him / to share /

(NAUSICAA bites her lip, shakes her head, and wounded by PINDAR's description, stares at the floor.)

And who could blame him? / She would have washed his linen / and his hair / then seeing how unclean his soul was / dragged it through his eyes / and running to some icy river / rinsed it / wrung it / wrung it / rinsed it / oh / such passionate laundry / So when she hung it out to dry it was fragile / flimsy / threadbare / and poor girl / staring at his cleansed soul / Nausicaa saw / nothing of Odysseus remained in there /

(An ugliness swamps PINDAR's beauty.)

THE FILTH THAT ENCRUSTED HIM WAS HIM /

(He creates a thin smile.)

Nausicaa / you are no longer fifteen / you are fifty-four / slender and exquisite / still / fifty-four / beware of your in / in / in /

(Again he parodies NAUSICAA. QUASIDOC cravenly shares his pleasure.)

INTRANSIGENCE /

(NAUSICAA allows their amusement to subside, then lifts her gaze.)

NAUSICAA: That you are a fraud / I have always known / that you are a poet / I have always doubted / but that you are prepared to use your poetry to justify your fraudulence /

(Exasperated and wounded at the same time, PINDAR cuts off NAUSICAA's rebuke.)

PINDAR: THAT YOU ARE / THAT YOU ARE /

NAUSICAA: I even / even I /

PINDAR: THAT YOU ARE / THAT YOU ARE / THAT / THAT / THAT /

(NAUSICAA recoils from his vehemence.)

I'LL GET POETRY AND SMACK YOUR ARSE WITH IT / I'LL ROLL UP POETRY AND GAG YOUR MOUTH WITH IT / WITH POETRY STICKS I'LL THRASH YOU ACROSS YOUR TITS / AND MAKING FISTS OF POETRY / I'LL BLACK YOUR EYES / YOU DAMNED BITCH / AND WHEN YOU'RE KILLED BY POETRY / I'LL DIG YOUR GRAVE WITH A POETRY SPADE / AND OVER YOUR GRAVE I'LL STICK A POETRY STONE / AND ON THE STONE IT WILL SAY THIS / IT WILL SAY /

(He is near to collapse.)

IT WILL SAY THIS /

(He staggers. He supports himself by clinging to one of the crates, which sways on its cables.)

She doubted Pindar was a poet /

23

A terrible chanting suffuses the stage. Knowing its source, QUASIDOC flings off her medical coat and flees. The old man edges on stage holding a black bag of medical appearance.

24

NAUSICAA goes to PINDAR as if to comfort him. Her raised hand is dashed away in a petulant gesture. She allows her hand to fall.

25

The chanting deepens. TOT is discovered holding a gun. Unfamiliar with it, he averts his face as he lifts it high and squeezes the trigger. The shot rings out. He winces.

26

BLOK: Her attitude to medicine is not informed by personal experience quite the contrary her life thus far has been characterized by perfect health headaches rare and coughs unknown those slight sensations of abnormality to which all men are prone she treats with water only water drinking substantial quantities from a pure source /

(NAUSICAA turns abruptly away from PINDAR and strides out. Suddenly she falls. She lies without moving.)

So it cannot be said as some have mischievously proposed that she suffered at some point in her life the ill-effects of clumsy surgery a scar perhaps or lingering discomfort which predisposes her to exact revenge oh no oh no /

(PINDAR recovers, and straightening himself, leaves without glancing at NAUSICAA. TOT in the meantime has levelled the gun, and no less apprehensive, discharges a second shot.)

27

BLOK: SHE KNOWS THE SICKNESS OF THE DOCTORS /

(He tips the bag. A cascade of scalpels. NAUSICAA climbs to her feet, brushes her skirt with one hand and marches out, passing TOT who advances downstage with the gun ineptly handled. BLOK inches off with the bag dangling from one hand.)

28

TOT: I went to Brady / Brady who rents weapons / twenty minutes / I said / twenty will do / from ten past / to half past one / at half past you will have it back / I promise you / cleaned / and a little warm perhaps / if used / but you know guns / how rarely a master shoots / gob does the job / some clever gob / some nimble hop / up on the counter / squashed chocolate / a spray of sherbet on your boots / mercy / mercy / says the shopman / edging back / don't move / I say / you effing piece of too-stiff cack / I'm mental / mercy / mental / see it in my eyes / take all you want boss / strip the till / strip the wife / I have this heart condition / too much stress and I / me too / I say / brain in my case / too much stress and I / two bare-faced liars in that little space / three with the missus dragging up her skirt / now it's me who begs for mercy / her sagging belly / her bulging eyes / mercy / I'll pull the trigger and call it self-defence / funny how the gun inspires / no stopping her / she's out to flash her dirt / like poetry / sets fire to things you'd never guess lay curled up in the dusty attics of their heads / chilled angels / clammy incubi /

(TOT laughs.)

TOO MUCH STRESS AND I /

(In his crazed ecstasy TOT looses off another shot. He jumps, then laughs again as the chanting crowd whose anthem has been a background to the last scenes, appears at the fringes of the stage.)

29

The crowd is at once silent. TOT's laugh drains away. BLOK continues his painful journey over the stage. Into the stillness, a medical trolley on squealing castors, a sound which counter-points the regular but laboured creaking of BLOK's soles. It is pushed by two impoverished men. On the trolley, aghast, a surgeon, half-erect but fixed by cords. The trolley stops. The surgeon's head turns, puppet-like, as he absorbs the spectacle. BLOK's soles creak. A sudden splash of anger.

LAMP: I cut the last of them / the last / I cut the last / me / me /

(Again, the silence. BLOK's soles, as he disappears offstage.)

SHEET: We all do / John /

LAMP: DO WE / DO WE /

RUBBER: The extermination of the doctors / John /

SHEET: He knows perfectly well /

RUBBER: Is a shared obligation /

SHEET: He knows / Michael /

RUBBER: It falls on all men equally /

LAMP: ON ALL MEN / BUT ESPECIALLY ME /

(Lamp lurches forward to snatch up one of the scalpels from the heap deposited by BLOK. Sensing his imminent destruction, the surgeon delivers a desperate oration.)

TRUCK: The annihilation of the doctors / the abolition of medicine / the demolition of the hospitals / the eradication of pharmaceutical encyclopaedia and text-books of anatomy / the liquidation of dentists / anaesthetists / opticians / chiropodists / and post-operative recuperation engineers / the spurious practitioners of pain relief / the dispensers of false hope / breast enlargers / face-changers / the cynical manipulators of love and vanity / critics of God

/ and self-appointed enemies of Death / I ASSENT TO IT / I
/ THE FINAL DOCTOR / CONFESS MY OWN BARBARITY /

*(TRUCK's desperate eloquence earns him a moment of silence, which
he times to his advantage. He lifts his head.)*

And I saved babies / WRONGLY /

(He turns his gaze from one of his persecutors to another.)

By my own skill I cut infant mortality by one hundred and
seventeen per cent /

(He roars.)

SKILL / SKILL /

(They seem almost afraid of TRUCK.)

PERVERSE MISAPPREHENSION /

(He tightens his fists.)

KILL ME / KILL THE ONE WHO CLAIMED TO KNOW THE
BONES AND BOWELS OF KINDNESS /

(His eyes challenge his audience. Again, he times his final appeal.)

Or let me go / and I will dig a field / not lifting my eyes
from the clay / and when they cry / from some place / a
man is hurt / I'll say /

(His mouth is like a gash.)

AH / SO THAT IS THAT / THEN /

*(The crowd is divided in its reaction to TRUCK's speech, some moved,
some sceptical.*

TOT: Good / good speech but slimy / slimy-good the speech /
I'd like to stay / bawling kill or mercy / but what a perfect
day for robbery /

LAMP: EIGHT TIMES THEY OPENED ME /

TOT: The corner shop / the post office / no queues / no witnesses /

LAMP: EIGHT TIMES THEIR PAWS IN ME /

TOT: And all the cops here / obviously /

LAMP: *(Tearing open his shirt.)* I SHOW / I SHOW /

TOT: *(Nimbly evading LAMP as he slips out.)* You tell 'em / pal /

LAMP: EIGHT AND STILL NOT HEALTHY /

PLATE: My baby died / all these sharp things inside her / like forks / like knives /

RUBBER: Sing / sing it / darling /

PLATE: Death wanted her / and you stuck forks in her / how is that kind? / A baby full of forks and skewers? /

RUBBER: Sing it / sing your rage / darling /

(The crowd takes up its chant. TRUCK senses his imminent destruction as the most eager surge forward to grab scalpels from the heap.)

30

BLOK is discovered retracing his steps. This time he carries a galvanized bucket in each hand.

BLOK: Profound consideration she gave to this decision / profound / I witnessed it / refusing food / and frowning / eat / madam / do eat I said / I will / I will / she muttered / her eyes staring from her head / profound consideration / eight days she fasted / no man who was well-fed made great decisions / profound / profound consideration /

31

LAMP, a scalpel held aloft, advances on the trolley.

LAMP: I'm opening the surgeon /

(TRUCK's guards tear away his medical coat, exposing his naked torso.)

RUBBER: Open him / John / open him /

SHEET: No scars / look / never cut / and never sewn /

PLATE: A locked house / is the surgeon /

RUBBER: Make doors in him / make doors and windows / John /

LAMP: I cut / I cut /

(The chant rises. The scalpel goes down. A look of horror spreads across TRUCK's features.)

The blood pours out / the light pours in /

RUBBER: Sing / surgeon / sing /

(LAMP stands away from his victim and tosses the scalpel into the bucket, now sufficiently close to make the gesture masterly. PLATE hurries forward and imitates his downward slash. The chant is fervid as individuals race to the victim, inflict wounds, and fling away the implements, which fall into the buckets with a ring. BLOK is patient, his gaze averted.)

32

The ritualistic character of the execution of TRUCK briefly obscures the reappearance of TOT, staggering, ashen and gunless.

SHEET: *(Appealing to TRUCK.)* Sing / oh sing the song of the last surgeon /

PLATE: Sing your pain / like me /

(She howls her words.)

Like / me /

(The last of the crowd wounds TRUCK, still upright on his knees. The chanting dies away. TRUCK, defiant or morbidly bemused, shakes

his head. The last scalpel rings in the bucket. The murderers watch TRUCK, who sways but slightly. BLOK proceeds, the sound of his squeaking soles a solitary accompaniment to the tension.)

RUBBER: He won't /

SHEET: He can't /

LAMP: He could /

RUBBER: He won't /

PLATE: He should /

RUBBER: He should / but will he? /

LAMP: For his own good /

PLATE: He should /

(She is resentful.)

He should /

(She walks strenuously to TRUCK.)

It kills the pain / it kills pain / poetry /

(TRUCK creates a contemptuous smile.)

KILLS IT NO / NOT KILLS IT/ NOT KILLS IT / NO /

(She searches. Her hands are wrung.)

It's a river / pain / you dam one stream it flows into another / so /

(She lifts a hand in her ordeal, and raising her eyes to the spectacle of TRUCK, gazes on him.)

You have your portion /

(The expression of contempt on TRUCK's face deepens.)

The poem / the poem /

(In her frustration PLATE turns an agonized face to TOT.)

Tot / oh / Tot / show him / show him what happens when pain meets the poem /

(TOT seems stricken.)

Does the poem / wash the wound / Tot? / Does it bandage it? /

(TOT is the focus of the crowd's rapt attention.)

Or disinfect / say /

(TOT writhes.)

It doesn't / does it / wash the blood away? /

(A peculiar laugh comes from TRUCK, his last.)

SAY IT FOR ME / TOT / I CAN'T /

(TOT, as if launched from a catapult, issues a stream of language that simultaneously plucks his body, a parody of a dance.)

TOT: Kick your heart over / kick it / the stone / the fence / the load of bricks that is your heart / the butchered bull / the distempered dog / the slippery toad that is your heart / kick it over / kick / and oh / what is this oozing stuff? / snot-thick and yellow / yellow as the eyes of magistrates / the flow of ten whores' holes / or newspapers in the bottom of a grave / but I'm not dead / oh say / say I'm not dead / tread / tread on your heart / ow / oh / no blood / no love / am I being killed or saved / empty now the kicked heart / cold and clean as snow / what made me walk so slowly / a convalescent in my own youth / I know now / oh I know / my heart was not my own / so kick your heart over / kick / kick /

(The song delivered, TOT is briefly still.)

I shot a bald shopkeeper / in Resurrection Street / and having done so / muttered sorry / was I sorry? / I wasn't / no /

(The crowd gawps.)

POL – ICE /

(He smiles thinly.)

The respect in which the Queen holds me is undiminished / so /

(He shrugs.)

POL – ICE /

(He shrugs.)

I've no dread /

(PLATE goes to TOT and kisses his cheek, a formality.)

33

The crowd drifts away. The sound of the winch.

34

TOT: POL – ICE /

35

EKO rises, as individuals linger, gazing at TOT before making their departure.

TOT: Police / I said / eventually / police came /

(NAUSICAA enters bearing a glass on a tray.)

But not in force / barely sufficient to contain a suspect who / had he the inclination / might easily have got away / I did not / however / have this inclination /

(NAUSICAA falls. The glass shatters and the tray slides.)

36

EKO arrives. She is motionless. BLOK appears, inching over the stage with a broom.

37

TOT: It was not awarded / then / the prize for poetry? / I think that's wise / if the poets fail to please you / by being / for example / inchoate / the thing would be diminished if it were awarded simply to alleviate some lout's poverty / on the other hand / I have to state / an insignificant shopkeeper's dead / and me / no more significant than him / could end up hanged / I won't be / obviously / your undiminished respect will / like some bucket of water / douse the flames of justice / indignation / and the rest / his wife tried to throttle me / but still / two nobodies dead / potentially / a pity / or not? / A pity / arguably? / And I took your advice / a post office / not a bank / but / trivial distinction / tell these blokes to go now / I'm free / free / funny word / the title of a poem / or several / free one / free two / I do variations / you know me / free three /

(He turns to the waiting officers.)

You can go now / boys / and many thanks for not beating me /

(He looks at EKO.)

They wanted to / of course / and hard / down steps / up steps / concrete and poets / they don't agree / so I mentioned your undiminished respect for me / mentioned did I say? / I bawled it / that did it / a miracle / have a seat / Tot / biscuit? / cup of tea? / I like the police / I'm perfectly sincere / I might have been a cop / I read the leaflets / but along came poetry / my ruination /

(He stares at EKO's unyielding back.)

Arguably /

(QUOTA marches in bearing a tray and glass.)

QUOTA: She says no /

TOT: Says no? / says no to what? / says no I was not ruined? /

(QUOTA stations herself alongside EKO.)

NAUSICAA: *(Rising to her feet.)* Murder / she says /

(She brushes down her dress in a perfunctory manner.)

Is punishable by death /

TOT: *(Indignant with dread.)* Yes / yes / everybody knows the penalty for /

NAUSICAA: Shh /

TOT: For murder is /

NAUSICAA: *(Straining to learn EKO's meaning.)* Shh /

(BLOK has arrived at the broken glass. He sweeps as NAUSICAA frowns with concentration.)

And do you dissent from this? /

TOT: Dissent? /

NAUSICAA: From the law? / do you quarrel with its stipulations? /

(TOT is haggard with dread.)

Its processes? / Its penalties? /

TOT: Not in the least / I say none of it relates to me /

(TOT's recklessness is met with silence, but for the creak of BLOK's boots as he withdraws the way he came.)

38

QUASIDOC, perched on a small-wheeled trolley, is pulled over the stage by PINDAR.

39

NAUSICAA: No / again / she says /

(Her attention is divided by the appearance of PINDAR.)

TOT: No what? / To what no? /

NAUSICAA: It's so in / so in /

TOT: TO WHAT NO? / ALL THIS NO / WHAT TO? /

NAUSICAA: *(Who is addressing PINDAR.)* SO IN / SOUCIANT / OF YOU /

QUOTA: No to your presumption / presumably /

PINDAR: *(Who has halted.)* My prize and I / we needed air / the staleness of the bedroom / unwashed linen / uncut hair / we were steeped in one another's / sore from one another's /

TOT: I say no to no /

PINDAR: *(Taunting NAUSICAA.)* ONE ANOTHER'S / ONE ANOTHER'S /

TOT: *(Turning violently.)* WHAT IS HE / THIS / THIS PRIZE-WINNER / WHAT IS HE DOING HERE? /

(QUASIDOC laughs. PINDAR smiles with the slightest contempt.)

40

BLOK is inching over the stage with dustpan and broom.

TOT: So I'm to hang / am I? / For a bald man in a post office / stains on his shirt / stains on his tie / and bitten fingernails / for this study in joylessness / I am to die? /

PINDAR: Forgive me asking / ha /

(He imitates frivolity.)

A question you may never ask / an idea you may never entertain / but what entitles you to more life than the bald man / whatever the condition of his nails? / Have you more right to life? /

(TOT regards PINDAR with withering contempt.)

TOT: You pimp of verse / of course I have /

PINDAR: *(With a superior gesture.)* He is certain of it / he /

NAUSICAA: *(Seething.)* FRAUD /

PINDAR: He is absolute in his conviction / he /

NAUSICAA: FRAUD /

PINDAR: He is immune to second thoughts /

(PINDAR smiles.)

QUOTA: Undress me / she says /

(TOT frowns.)

TOT: Un /

QUOTA: Dress me / yes /

(TOT hangs his head. QUASIDOC laughs, and stops. TOT, reluctantly, goes to QUOTA and begins to unfasten her clothes. He stops.)

TOT: I think I /

QUOTA: NOW / SHE IS IMPATIENT / NOW SHE SAYS /

(BLOK sweeps up the glass as TOT makes QUOTA naked. He goes to touch her. He is stricken with despair. EKO sings.)

EKO: I stand / trembling as a tethered mare / I stand / and the winds like maids of matrimony lift my hair in their fingers / I dare not meet your gaze / I dare not / for fear it is ferocious /

(TOT is a study in impotence. BLOK's shoes creak as he departs.)

TOT: CAN'T /

EKO: My pale skin shivvers like the surface of a mere / when
draughts lap its surface / oh / my dear / am I too naked /
have I wounded you with beauty? / A witch of brutal ways
might move you more / how I / so sweetly educated / long
to hear a cascade of obscenity pour from your mouth /

TOT: CAN'T /

(He flings away from QUOTA.)

CAN'T / WHO COULD / NOBODY / NOBODY COULD /
NOBODY COULD / NOT WITH A / COULD YOU? /

(He turns to the officers.)

FUCK WITH / COULD YOU / PAL / FUCK WITH A DEATH
SENTENCE? / I'LL TRY AGAIN /

(He goes to return to QUOTA, who is restoring her clothing.)

NAUSICAA: Too late / she says /

(EKO has taken the glass from the tray and sips.)

TOT: DON'T TOP A POET FOR A SHOPKEEPER /

*(EKO seems not to heed TOT's appeal. PINDAR picks up the ropes
of the trolley.)*

PINDAR: Some part of me / a small part / admittedly / envies
you / Tot / I have this little gauge inside my head / don't
you? / which registers the pressure of my jealousy / and
the needle/ swings into the red to contemplate your place /
not in the present / but in history /

NAUSICAA: That isn't fraudulent /

PINDAR: What does it matter / the quality of your art / or
the state of your conscience? / all that schoolchildren will
know of Tot is that he perished on the scaffold / easy-won
his reputation / whereas me / the small things I achieved /

NAUSICAA: THAT IS /

PINDAR: In a long life / possibly / will show only from deep and conscientious study /

NAUSICAA: VERY FRAUDULENT / INDEED /

PINDAR: *(Stung.)* NAUSICAA / I AM TAKING LEAVE OF A FELLOW ARTIST FOR WHOM /

(BLOK, not yet offstage, drops the dustpan, which clatters, the glass shards ringing on the floor.)

QUOTA: She says silence / silence / everyone /

PINDAR: *(To TOT.)* I hope it doesn't hurt /

QUOTA: SILENCE / SHE SAYS /

PINDAR: *(Adamant.)* I DO / I DO HOPE IT'S A PAINLESS / HANGING

(A cold silence endures.)

QUOTA: *(Frowning to discern.)* Why? /

(QUOTA turns her head as if to catch EKO's meaning.)

Why / she says / do you hope it's painless? /

(For the first time, BLOK emits a long laugh. PINDAR's fingers twitch in an embarrassment. The two police draw their overcoats together and button them, as if to set off with their charge.)

41

NAUSICAA: *(Frowning as she interprets EKO.)* It is not the length of life / it is the in / in /

(Her head twirls in her struggle.)

The intensity / she says /

(EKO replaces the empty glass on the tray. The winch commences. EKO begins her descent.)

TOT: *(A final bid.)* SHE CARES FOR ME /

QUOTA: *(Leaving smartly with the tray.)* That's obvious to everybody /

TOT: CARES FOR ME SO /

(The two police advance on TOT, who seems to decay.)

Cares / cares / do you know that word / cares? /

I think cares must mean /

(He is suddenly rigid.)

DON'T LAY HANDS ON ME / NO NEED FOR GAGS / HOODS / BRACELETS /

(He begs EKO.)

TELL THEM NO BITS / SOME GO TO EXECUTION WITH THEIR HANDS FREE / LET ME / SWIFTLY WITH A SMILE / A CRAZED SMILE ON THEIR LIPS / OH /

(He is stopped by a thought which causes him to tremble with a silent laugh.)

Oh / to care for / to care for must mean this /

(He gnaws a finger.)

That Tot be Tot / and all that is not Tot be lifted from him / a weight of habit that his slender shoulders cannot bear / and what is shallow-Tot be abolished / so deeper-Tot can swim up out of darkness like a great fish / bawling his name and filling his unused lungs with air /

(EKO is sinking from sight. TOT rushes to see her head drawn down.)

IS THAT WHAT CARING IS? / YOU DARE TO LET THE LOVED ONE /

(He runs his fingers over his own face.)

Hang? / if hanging is what /

43

(He laughs peculiarly.)

Describes him? /

(The sound of BLOK with dustpan and broom.)

PINDAR: No one will know / this surely is the privilege
accorded those who die young / that never in a thousand
years could they have done what early signs / like palsied
fingers pointing to a dawn / a dawn that mercifully cannot
ever come / so rashly predicted / I envy you / oh / many
things I envy you / Tot / but nothing more than this / this /
immunity / from a severe and mature judgement /

BLOK: *(Unbending painfully.)* He's not hanging / he's got seven
years /

(He bangs the broom against the dustpan, the habit of a domestic.)

42

*TOT weakens at the knees. The police rush forward to catch him in
his faint.*

QUASIDOC: So near / me too / we two / so very proximate /
thank you / we say / another day / in sixty languages / the
language of the blood / the liver / and the bone / ow shout
the lungs / the whispered merci / merci / of the brain /
the cunt lips say their slippery slogans / pressed together /
pray /

TOT: *(Separating the police.)* I'M NOT /

QUASIDOC: Pray like novices /

TOT: HAPPY /

(He thinly smiles.)

With this information /

(He spins.)

How accurate is it / anyway / this seven years / seven / was it? / Seven / did he say? / It could be torture / condemned / reprieved / dragged up the scaffold / dragged down again / lawyers / verdicts / postponements / and delays of thirty years / I was composing my last testament / TOT'S CHEERIO / in fifteen lines /

(He turns to the police.)

You would have liked it / no unkind things about the law /

(He splutters.)

I'M NOT SURE IF I WANT MORE OF THIS /

(He creates a gesture.)

THIS /

(TOT's grand manner fills PINDAR with contempt. He averts his gaze.)

Restore the penalty / Tot can't stand Tot / you see / it hurts to be him / to wake with Tot / to fall asleep with him / no one knows his agony /

(If the police are moved to pity, PINDAR is derisive.)

PINDAR: Now who's the fraud? /

(PINDAR goes to draw the trolley away. TOT seethes.)

TOT: I will murder you for that /

POLICE: Steady / son /

PINDAR: Yes / steady /

TOT: Because / oh /

(He shakes his head.)

PINDAR: Because you are a fraud / and because I said so / you will murder me /

TOT: No /

PINDAR: Do be careful / Tot /

TOT: Not that / no /

PINDAR: *(Going to leave again.)* It's habit-forming / murder / and I'm no /

TOT: DON'T GO / I SAID /

PINDAR: *(Stopping.)* NO BALD SHOP-KEEPER /

(The poets glare at one another.)

TOT: You were correct to call me fraudulent / I was / I yielded to it / and for one reason only / you were my audience /

(TOT aches.)

AND I DESPISE YOU /

(He lifts his hands in bewilderment.)

You corrupt us / and that is why I will do / one day / what I said I'd do /

(He looks to the police.)

And you / take note of it /

43

TOT's defiant stare turns into one of mischief. Without a hint of his intention, he suddenly makes to bolt. The police are equally nimble and trap him. One forces him onto his knees. The other clamps handcuffs on his wrists.

NAUSICAA: In / in / in / tegral to the poem she knows one day you will write / is this seven years' in / in / in / carceration / Mr Tot / she has not the slightest interest in justice / as you may know / you might have shot a dozen shop-keepers / and set light to their children/ in / in / in / iquity / is the poet's right / so long as it makes poetry / so she is dipping you in prison / head first but holding tightly to one ankle /

(The police lift TOT.)

Oh /

(They stop.)

And she adds / a contradiction / surely? / avoid all fights /

(TOT regards NAUSICAA with a sour expression. NAUSICAA gazes at the floor.)

44

The crates of dead doctors plunge through the floor with a crash. The police rush TOT offstage, his feet barely touching the floor.

45

NAUSICAA: I think you two / just looking / just looking at the pair of you / I think /

(She seems unable to express herself.)

BLOK: *(Who has not moved since last speaking.)* I'll say / shall I? / I'll /

NAUSICAA: I'm not in / in / in /

BLOK: I'll say it /

NAUSICAA: I'M NOT IN / HIBITED /

BLOK: You're not / you're not inhibited / but I can say it better /

(NAUSICAA concedes with a slight move of her head.)

Looking at the pair of you / she thinks / these two belong / in what way? / in this way /

NAUSICAA: They /

BLOK: Are confined /

NAUSICAA: They /

BLOK: As dogs are by fences /

NAUSICAA: They /

BLOK: Pace /

NAUSICAA: They /

BLOK: Tread / by night and day / even in their sleep /

NAUSICAA: They /

BLOK: Dream of defending the small ground of their /

NAUSICAA: ODYSSEUS WAS THE SAME /

(NAUSICAA's fists clench. BLOK concedes.)

No matter what you showed him / of passion / or extravagance / thrusting underneath his nose the scents of naivety or of decay / he had a single destination /

(She bites her lip.)

And this gift he had / oh / the exquisite gift of mischief / merely served to hasten him to where he was / in any case / already going /

(She seems to smile.)

The lie is beautiful / but only when it serves to in / in / in /

(Now she trembles with rage at her inadequacy.)

In /

BLOK: *(Helpfully.)* Inspire? /

NAUSICAA: *(Irritably.)* I HAVE TO SAY / ME / ME / ME / I HAVE TO SAY /

(BLOK inclines his head.)

Only when it /

(She seems calm.)

INITIATES /

(She is relieved to have uttered.)

New life /

(She regards PINDAR coolly.)

The poem is a lie / but why lie at all / if lying serves only to /

(NAUSICAA suffers in her effort to articulate.)

To /

(They watch NAUSICAA in her ordeal. PINDAR goes towards her.)

PINDAR: I am a prize-winner / Nausicaa /

(The statement seems to drain NAUSICAA of her agony, replacing pain with incomprehension.)

Not once / not twice / but again / and again / and again /

(NAUSICAA sways on her feet.)

So are the judges / and the people / and the queen / insane? /

(QUASIDOC, on her trolley, laughs with admiration, a scalding to NAUSICAA.)

NAUSICAA: I will never / obviously / be naked with you again / and just as my body will / forever possibly / stay unexposed / so will those things I struggled to / and invariably failed to / drag into the light of day /

(She lifts her head.)

When at last I do explain myself / it will not be for your hearing /

(A pitiful smile hangs on her lips.)

Your cleverness kills you / Pindar / and it was / oh / entirely vain of me / to think I might have rescued you from cleverness /

(PINDAR inclines his head sarcastically.)

You lose my gnawing criticism / and you gain a doctor's laugh /

PINDAR: *(Savagely.)* PREFERRED / PREFERRED /

NAUSICAA: Yes /

PINDAR: IN / IN / IN / FINITELY PREFERRED /

(PINDAR seizes the ropes of the trolley and sweeps offstage. BLOK observes NAUSICAA, dustpan in one hand, broom in the other.)

NAUSICAA: Darling / yes / yes / darling /

(She squirms.)

BLOK: I'll finish what I was saying / about the two dogs / the two dogs and the fence /

NAUSICAA: *(Oblivious to BLOK.)* Yes / darling / yes / yes / darling / yes /

BLOK: The metaphor of trodden ground / which / so trodden and so small / in area / and circumference / by this incessant treading / becomes a mess /

(NAUSICAA collapses, and twitches violently over the floor.)

NAUSICAA: DARLING / DARLING /

BLOK: The dogs / being dogs / being therefore /

NAUSICAA: DARLING /

BLOK: Confined themselves / inside the painful perimeter of canine intelligence /

NAUSICAA: *(Screaming.)* DAR – LING /

BLOK: Can no more imagine a territory outside the fence than we / semi-cultured / semi-decadent / can dream a landscape beyond the spiked railings of our own kindness /

NAUSICAA: DAR – LNG /

BLOK: We tread / we shit / we tread in our own shit /

NAUSICAA: DAR – LING / DAR – LING /

BLOK: *(Inflamed.)* I'M SHITTING /

NAUSICAA: DAR – LING /

BLOK: I'M TREADING /

NAUSICAA: OH DAR – LING / DAR – LING /

BLOK: I'M SHITTING AND I'M TREADING / OH / THE SMELL / THE CLINGING /

NAUSICAA: DAR – LING / OH /

(She rolls, her weeping gaining on her speaking.)

Oh /

BLOK: THE SHITTING AND THE TREADING OF THE SHIT /

NAUSICAA: *(Slowly ceasing.)* Oh / Oh /

BLOK: *(Also more calm.)* Oh / the ordure / the smothered dogs / poor dogs / in ordure / smothered / dogs / dogs / pitiful / the encrusted dogs /

(NAUSICAA is still. BLOK also. As if to resume his duties, he lifts the dustpan, but stops.)

Mr Pindar / stinking somewhat / howls on a windy night / his verse / like Mr Pindar /

(He thinks. His mouth moves silently.)

In faeces / plods /

(He contemplates the picture, then abandons it.)

How hard it is to be naked / I so / so deeply felt it / when you said /

(His shoulders lift, and fall.)

You found it / hard / nakedness /

NAUSICAA: *(Still lying, and quite still.)* Oh / Blok / do you know / I sometimes sing your poetry? /

BLOK: Yes / and /

(He looks down.)

Do you know / I sometimes steal your underwear? /

NAUSICAA: Yes /

BLOK: And kiss it? /

NAUSICAA: Yes /

(They seem to reflect. BLOK taps the broom against the dustpan, as if to discipline his thought.)

BLOK: That is perfection / is it not? / You sing me / and I kiss what / if it is no longer warm from your body / is full of your fragrance / I call that in /

(He looks at her, his mimicry in contra-distinction to PINDAR's, kind.)

in / in / timacy /

46

NAUSICAA stands. She goes towards BLOK. She falls and is quite still. BLOK observes the collapsed form of NAUSICAA, himself quite still, before leaving.

47

Squalls and showers sweep the stage. NAUSICAA's clothing flaps in the draughts.

48

Sickly or aged individuals stagger on sticks, sinking and rising or not rising. Those prone or prostrate lift pitiful hands. All are naked. If they mutter, it is barely audible in the susurrating winds. The chill arouses NAUSICAA, who sits up and observes the spectacle, half-fascinated, half-horrified. At last, no movement can be discerned in the condemned.

49

The wind dies. Birdsong and warm light. EKO, swaythed in furs, is pushed on-stage by QUOTA. Some distance behind, men with spades form a group.

QUOTA: The thaw / the never-lovely thaw / she says / as if / as if / the thing that we implore must / by some cruel law / be / as if / as if / the longer we waited / the more deep our disappointment / necessarily / she says / of you / you / Nausicaa / a certain indignation / how can you march about in winter / with no boots? / She is emphatic / have you no boots? / Answer /

(NAUSICAA seems to gather her resources. EKO flings a fur at her, which NAUSICAA catches.)

NAUSICAA: Icy is the hospital /

50

BLOK, clad for winter, advances over the field with a tray and a glass.

51

NAUSICAA: I saw a hare /

QUOTA: The boot question /

NAUSICAA: The hare was poised /

BLOK: Poised hare /

QUOTA: About the boots /

NAUSICAA: As if it were suspended /

BLOK: Slung /

NAUSICAA: Or slung from wires so fine as to be invisible /

QUOTA: Do you possess a pair / and simply /

BLOK: Slung hare /

QUOTA: Forgot to wear them? /

NAUSICAA: As if these dead had beckoned him /

BLOK: Beckoned hare /

NAUSICAA: To utter silently /

BLOK: Silently uttering hare /

QUOTA: She will buy you boots in suede or leather /

NAUSICAA: The wonder and despair /

QUOTA: Say / please /

NAUSICAA: Of dying /

BLOK: Profoundly privileged hare /

> (BLOK *proceeds over the thaw towards EKO. NAUSICAA pulls the* *fur tight.*)

NAUSICAA: I have boots / I / I merely /

52

EKO sings.

EKO: No sound but the crows' lament for love / my killed
excellence / how still the mountain / even the glacier / for
a single night / groaned hardly / hardly / .

(BLOK arrives with the tray. EKO takes the glass and drinks. A figure, pitiful in poor clothing, is discovered.)

53

TOT: I got ill /

(He coughs, deeply and painfully.)

And lost an arm /

(He looks up.)

Anybody interested? /

(No one responds, but all are aware.)

The arm / a machine ate it / in the prison workshop / blood on the ceiling / splash / like a show-off's signature / and no doctors /

(He sniffs.)

It was touch and go /

As for the lungs / oh / eight in a cell / and no ventilation / CORRECTION /

(He half-smiles.)

There was ventilation / but we stuffed it up with newspapers / so / if one of you was even slightly ill / no one escaped it / I don't complain / it eats me / it eats me as if each lung was a nest of rodents / eaten from the outside / eaten from within / to generalize from these particulars / I would have to say / when Tot was released from prison / there was a lot less Tot than when Tot went in /

(He looks at the ground.)

I don't complain /

QUOTA: She says /

(QUOTA strains to interpret the silence of EKO.)

Submit a poem / Mr Tot /

(BLOK begins his withdrawal with the tray. The workmen advance as if signalled and dig graves.)

54

The music of the shovels. Rooks caw. EKO is drawn away by QUOTA.

NAUSICAA: *(To TOT, who is motionless.)* Wear this /

(She extends the fur given her by EKO. TOT looks peculiarly at NAUSICAA.)

Wear this / why don't you? /

(TOT tacitly denies her.)

She thinks / you know I think / poetry is not made but crushed / crushed out of extremity / the poet therefore / how hard this is to say to you / must perish / must perish as a consequence of his own /

TOT: *(Gazing at the dead.)* Cold's kind /

(NAUSICAA is rebuked, but determined.)

NAUSICAA: I agree with this / but if the poet's dead / then /

TOT: He's silent /

(TOT is suddenly animated.)

SILENT / AND ALL THE BEST / THE THINGS HE NEVER PUT ON PAPER /

(He hurries to a corpse and lifts up the head with his remaining arm.)

TRAPPED / TRAPPED /

(He appears to jerk the dead man's head. The workmen are indignant.)

WORKMAN: Oi / oi /

TOT: IN DARK CORRIDORS / IN DAMP VAULTS /

WORKMAN: Oi / I said /

TOT: *(Obedient.)* All right / all right /

(He stands. He wipes his hand on his decayed garments.)

The old man / Blok / who carries trays / I did not expect to see again / but some great song is running in his head / until it's written /

(He stops.)

I'll have the stole /

(He looks about him.)

The dead will have to wait for their great interpreter /

(NAUSICAA goes to TOT, and extends the stole. Suddenly she seems seized.)

NAUSICAA: Will you be / oh / will you / will you be / will you be all we / all we / please be / be / BE / BE / TOT / BE /

(She stares with a terrible desperation. TOT feels the weight of the world descend onto his shoulders, and nearly flinches. NAUSICAA turns and strides away, but recollecting she is still holding the fur, turns and tosses it. TOT catches it in his single hand. NAUSICAA goes.)

55

The dead are interred to the music of the spades, which ring in the frosty air. Rooks complain. Men cough, unhealthily. TOT's arm remains outstretched.

TOT: Excessively alive / the one-armed man / the ruthless and religious rhetoric / of the recidivist / wreck you / wreck you / of course I do / in the hope department / in the hope shop / in the hope house / pulling it out / rope or gut / you say / darling / you say / the reeking bowel / one thousand yards of / and like the dinner in the vagrants' kitchen steaming / steaming the dreaming / entrails /

56

The dead are buried, the workmen, shouldering their tools, march off the empty field. PINDAR, exquisite in winter fashions, is discovered observing TOT, whose hand, outstretched, becomes an object of study to TOT himself.

PINDAR: I think that's true / that hope resides not in those places associated with intelligence / but as you suggest / in dark and stubborn places / is visceral / therefore /

(TOT ignores PINDAR.)

Those six poems /

(He shakes his head.)

What a six / I said to her / that six / that lovely six / reward him /

(TOT is examining the limb.)

For God's sake / award the prize / the man is / oh / I was humorous / unwise with her / DISFIGURED BY INGRATITUDE / it didn't work / so I resorted to superlatives / saying the six were / so this / so that / so very / which damned you further in her eyes /

(PINDAR half-laughs.)

I apologize / probably you squirm to think I urged on your behalf /

(TOT ignores PINDAR, which drives PINDAR to reckless confession.)

So it's me again /

(TOT is motionless.)

AM I THAT GOOD? / I ASK YOU / IS IT POSSIBLE I CAN / YEAR UPON YEAR / CREATE THINGS OF SUCH

EXCELLENCE I AM / NOT ONLY FAVOURED / BUT
ACTUALLY / ENTITLED / TO THIS / HA / I NEARLY
CALLED IT AVALANCHE / BUT AN AVALANCHE IS / BY
DEFINITION / SUDDEN / AND CEASES SUDDENLY /
NOT AVALANCHE THEREFORE / TORRENT RATHER /
PERPETUAL TORRENT OF PRIZES? /

(Allowing his arm to fall at last, TOT turns to face PINDAR.)

No / I think it's not my excellence / if excellent I am / let
the world dispute my excellence / but this peculiar / and /
oh / far from comfortable I assure you / noise in my head /
a traffic / a traffic / yes / which /

(He ceases, sensing TOT holds him in contempt.)

I'll finish /

(He looks into TOT with a similar intensity.)

Through your yellow loathing / through your red spite /
the traffic of my time / it roars in me / I am / condemned
/ you'd say / to be the speaker of my day / there / I live
in luxury / while you / how ill you look / Tot / while you
decay in verminous clothing / can I give you something?
/ Money? / Silly / silly to offer / silly / weak and offensive
gesture / I know what you'll say / so don't say it / for some
reason / Tot /

(PINDAR's smile is sickly.)

I wanted to /

(His hands move uncomfortably.)

But really / you're just unlucky /

(He rages.)

YOU'RE NOT A SAINT / YOU'RE NOT AN ANGEL /
NEITHER AN ANGEL NOR A SAINT /

(The two men stare.)

Just a box of circumstances / OH / I DROPPED THE BOX /
clatter / clatter / spoons / forks / and bent coins /

(Again he smiles the sickly smile.)

TOT: You are so much better when you hate / but you hate to
hate / now give me the money you think I should fling in
your face /

*(PINDAR seems to contemplate the request. Then he reaches into the
depths of his coats and removes his wallet. He extends the wad of
notes. TOT declines to step up to PINDAR, obliging PINDAR to move
towards him, a cruel manipulation PINDAR understands well and
which causes him to smile for the first time authentically.)*

57

*The currency links them, held by both men but the property of neither.
As if ignited, they roar a cacophony.*

TOT: *(Simultaneous with PINDAR.)* HOWLING AND / SWEATING
AND / THE MOON PRESENTS / AN UNWASHED FACE TO
YOU / NO STAR IN YOUR PASTEL BEDROOM / NO NAKED
STAR / NO FROZEN CUNTED AND CELESTIAL / OR DOG
OUT OF THE FIELDS / PISS CLANGING OFF HIS FLANKS
IN ICICLES / OR GIRLS OF TWELVE / NO / NO / THEIR
BONES EXPLODING FROM THEIR ARSES / MOON SHE /
MOON SHE / IN FALLING SOCKS / SCREAMS LAUGHING
/ HIS SO-DISCREET / POISONS / DISCOVER ME / SPREAD
/ CHEAPLY SPREAD / BENEATH A DINNER TABLE WITH A
SICK MENU / A SICK MENU /

PINDAR: *(Simultaneous with TOT.)* MOTHER / MOTHER / IN
BAWLING SHEETS OF STARCH AND BLEACH / AND STEAM
/ AND TIN / UP / UP ON MY TIN TABLE / YOU SHRUNKEN
BASTARD / YOUR FILTHY KNEES OF DREAD / UNDER
ANAEMIC LIGHTS OF POVERTY I SEE / I SEE THE MOUTH
OF DRUDGERY IS DUMB/ HANG US / WITH WIRE / BURN
OUR NECKS UNDER THE MURDERED TREES OF NATIONS
/ OLD AND LOST NATIONS / SCRAPS / RAGS / THEY RISE

UP / OH / JACQUERIE / JACQUERIE / THE POET HAS PALE
ELBOWS / RIEN QUE / RIEN QUE JACQUERIE /

*(As they lose energy the words fall out slower, the syllables grind
to a silence, the wad of notes remaining aloft until at last PINDAR
releases his grip. BLOK is seen edging on stage.)*

58

*TOT draws the fur round himself and hurries off. PINDAR observes
the painful motions of BLOK, his hands opening and closing in an
anxiety. BLOK transports a chair.*

PINDAR: Bring back medicine /

(BLOK ignores him.)

I don't say this for myself / you understand / I am in
perfect health /

(Still BLOK seems not to hear him.)

Perfect health / but others / others / they / and you / your
bones / if I may say so / have their own opinions about
which way you're going /

*(PINDAR cannot resist laughing at his own joke. BLOK stops. He
does not lift his gaze to PINDAR.)*

BLOK: Do you want to live forever / Mr Pindar? /

PINDAR: I don't think it is a question of /

(He provokes BLOK.)

Yes / I think I do /

BLOK: And have you not accumulated sufficient testimony
to your gifts in poetry but you require to be heaped
with more prizes / Mr Pindar? / More rewards? /
More uncritical applause? / Some say the flame of your
originality will suffocate beneath the weight of this
unprecedented approbation / I'm old / of course / old /

perverse / and with a heart that trembles like a glass on a tin table / every tram that passes sets it shaking / but death is kind / and even / yes / contrary to popular opinion / discriminating / you need death / Mr Pindar / to save your reputation /

(He offers PINDAR a cruel smile.)

You know this / which is why you never sleep at night / life is as long as it needs to be / Mr Pindar / tell your wet doctor / your wet / wet doctor / so full of fuck she is / when you cry your last cry / no drug / no knife / darling /

(The old man chokes on his humour, sniffs, recovers.)

PINDAR: And you / sweet-sleeping old man who wears dogs as blankets / what might put a term to you? /

BLOK: Me? / Oh / I've one more song to write /

PINDAR: Don't keep us waiting /

(He glares at BLOK, and swiftly repudiates himself.)

THAT WAS UGLY / AND STUPID / AND UGLY / AND UGLY / AND UGLY / you are / SO UGLY / a poet of /

(He shakes his head.)

IMMENSITY / FORGIVE MY UGLINESS / BLOK / OH / FORGIVE IT /

(BLOK is surprised to see PINDAR sink under his own tears. PINDAR's arms wave pathetically in the air, as if he drowned.)

59

The sound of the winch. EKO is lifted through the stage.

BLOK: He wonders where the song is / this song / this so / this much / this oft / this highly / this / where is the song / he says / not saying it / but /

(QUOTA enters swiftly as BLOK places his chair some yards from EKO.)

And the anticipation / that alone imposes / that of itself commands / extreme /

(He sits.)

He called me dog-smothered / he called me dog-wrapped / it's true / I'm all /

(He makes gestures of brushing his waistcoat.)

QUOTA: *(As EKO appears slowly.)* She says not dog-wrapped /

(BLOK ceases brushing.)

NOT DOG-WRAPPED / SHE INSISTS /

BLOK: No / no / strictly speaking / it was not him said /

QUOTA: No / it wasn't / she laughs /

BLOK: It was me said dog-wrapped /

QUOTA: He couldn't / she says / he could never have said dog-wrapped / it's your line / she says / laughing / your line and he is / he is /

(QUOTA waits.)

AN ARCTIC WASTE OF MEDIOCRITY /

BLOK: Yes /

(EKO has arrived and stares ahead.)

Yes / he is /

(A silence falls, near-tangible.)

60

BLOK, as if unfamiliar with the seated position, is uncomfortable. His fingers twirl. EKO gazes ahead, but not in his direction.

QUOTA: *(At last.)* The chair / move it / she says /

BLOK: *(Rising stiffly.)* Move it / yes /

QUOTA: You're too near /

BLOK: Near / am I? /

QUOTA: Too near and /

(QUOTA frowns with the effort of interpretation.)

She requires to see you / so /

(BLOK manoeuvres himself and the chair.)

Further away but / in her line of sight / please / please / she says /

(BLOK places the chair.)

Darling / that's nice / sit / darling / sit /

(BLOK is obedient. He studies EKO. He folds his hands on his knees.)

Referring to this song / this so / this much / this highly / this / she is /

(QUOTA is refined in her interpretations.)

Not sarcastic / but quoting you / this so / this much / this highly anticipated song / she says you know perfectly well the reasons that are / she is employing metaphor / the shoulder that is leaning on the door /

(QUOTA frowns with effort.)

Is hers / she / she / she prevents you / she inhibits the singing of this so / this much / etcetera / anticipated song /

(BLOK goes to dismiss the suggestion.)

More / shh / more /

(He is silenced.)

By clinging to a life that / once ended / will cause to /

(She shakes her head with the effort of interpretation.)

Flourish / to / erupt / in your ancient and / dusty / head / exotic metaphors and unexpected rhyme / as if / in an abandoned city / up shot gardens / pendulous and / fragrant / but /

(She aches.)

She must be dead / look in her eyes /

(BLOK appears afraid.)

LOOK IN HER EYES / SHE SAYS /

(BLOK looks at EKO.)

Darling / darling / darling again /

(QUOTA is silent as BLOK and EKO observe one another.)

Make love / she says /

(QUOTA goes to leave them.)

Make love /

61

BLOK stares into EKO, and the gaze is resolute. TOT is discovered observing them, but motionless. BLOK, clumsy with age, rises to his feet, toppling his chair, which clatters.

TOT: Blok / Eko /

(BLOK gazes, quite still.)

BLOK / EKO / THE NAMES / THEY SLOT TOGETHER / Even if they didn't want to / surely they were condemned to fuck? / A LINGUISTIC OBLIGATION / Eros nothing / sound alone would twist two lawyers into the act / two criminals / two monkeys / it's a fact / words set your knees trembling / things ooze inside you / strings crack / and Blok was a poet / thin with the poison of his poetry / and Eko / the daughter of a maniac / a despot / a king / she got all that / SWEET SAVAGERY / from him / contemplating

torture / from a bed / gasping at beheadings / the poet's
finger swimming in her womb / and her digits / nimble
as the potter who swirls tall pots from clay / raising the
undreamed phallus out of him / all poets are dictators /
and dictators / they would sing / and how she sang / it
was her second excellence / her arse the first / oh / arse of
arses / the lungs of Blok / they burst to see it stripped / on
palace balconies in sunshine / or down sweet alleys where
they trespassed for a filthy thing / a web of nothing was
her underwear / and his poet's trousers / wide to swing his
trapezing dogbits in /

*(NAUSICAA has entered with two glasses on a tray, but falls, the
glasses shattering, the tray sliding over the floor. BLOK, infatuated,
advances on EKO, who receives him in her mouth.)*

Can this last forever / Darling? / Let me be your slave /

BLOK: DARLING / DARLING /

*(The old man's hands lift slowly as crows, and hang in the air. TOT
lights a cigarette, the flash of his lighter illuminating his shadowy
presence. NAUSICAA is utterly still on the floor.)*

62

Deep sobs come from BLOK. His right hand sweetly holds EKO's head.

63

TOT: I couldn't write for five years /

(BLOK slowly removes himself from EKO.)

Noise /

*(BLOK lifts EKO's hand and places it against his forehead, as if
blessed by her.)*

Two noises / to be precise /

(The old man edges away, picking up his chair and setting off.)

Gaol noise / the racket of / the banging and the howling / and then / worse still / the noise of scum conversing / I'm scum / obviously / you'd think / scum's immune to scum chatter? / The opposite / malheureusement / that little room / three scum / scum chatter multiplied by three / triple scum chatter / my brain took offence / malheureusement / pulled down its hat / turned its back on me / I did French classes / some mad bitch with piled-up hair and a degree / killers thrilled her / the worse the better / her stuff trickled to her knee / aimes-toi la violence? / and Russian / and Chinese characters / I said I was a poet / so could I run the library? / malheureusement / non / the job was taken / a financier with seven yachts / seven? / oui / seven / Tot / he said / never read a novel / only read the dictionary / excellent advice / which is why I know the word INCHOATE / I'm going back eight years / never should have been applied to me/ do you like the new ones? /

(BLOK has disappeared. EKO is silent and still.)

The cycle in hexameters? /

(There is no response.)

Oddly conservative / some might say /

(The silence persists.)

For one who lost an arm / a lung / and half his brain in prison / I don't mean thematically / the form / the form is /

NAUSICAA: *(Still prostrate.)* Two she likes / the fifth / and the eleventh / yes to those / the rest /

(She sits up.)

In / in /

(NAUSICAA disciplines her voice.)

IN / TEMPERATE / SHE SAYS /

TOT: *(In utter despair.)* Intemperate /

(TOT's single hand crushes the air.)

NAUSICAA: When she spoke / on the last occasion / of intensification / she did not mean more / she meant deeper /

(TOT shakes his head, utterly defeated. With a crash, the winch begins.)

Her confidence in you is undiminished /

(EKO begins her descent. TOT makes a desperate bid for salvation.)

TOT: CAN I HAVE A PRIZE / PLEASE? / ANY PRIZE / OR IF NOT A PRIZE A PENSION? / I AM SO / SO /

(TOT's head twists in his agony.)

NAUSICAA: She knows the full extent of your poverty /

(TOT is simultaneously injured and bewildered. He stares at the descending form of EKO. As BLOK begins to sweep the broken glass, EKO sings.)

EKO: Upstairs / beyond the dark landings / and the umbrella stand / my sinful room smiles like a lynx /

(TOT is shocked to hear his own words sung. BLOK departs.)

I smell the pungent odour of your hesitation /

TOT: That's mine /

EKO: Your eyes / too heavy to be lifted / sink / sink down your cheeks /

TOT: That's mine / she's singing /

EKO: *(Nearly disappeared now.)* Blindly you walk in / warm as an athlete who has run beyond the field of shame /

TOT: *(Advancing on EKO.)* MY OWN / THAT / TOT'S / SHE SINGS ME AND /

(TOT splutters with indignation.)

THE QUEEN SINGS TOT / AND TOT /

(BLOK, returning with the dustpan and broom in his usual fashion, disciplines TOT by beating the broom on the pan.)

HE'S STARVING /

64

BLOK sweeps the broken glass into the dustpan. TOT laughs, in a deadly fashion. It ends. BLOK edges away.

NAUSICAA: It doesn't matter / if you starve or not /

(TOT is still, as if he had not heard her.)

Dinnerless / so what? / and shirt in shreds / irrelevant however / irrelevant the material condition of the poet Tot /

(She gazes at him, biting her lip.)

TOT: I have one arm /

NAUSICAA: *(Interpreting his statement as evidence of hope.)* One / yes /

TOT: And one hand /

NAUSICAA: *(Radiant.)* One / yes / with which to grasp a pen when passion or despair inspires you /

TOT: ONE HAND TO SMACK YOUR FACE WITH /

(NAUSICAA accepts TOT's rebuke. Slowly she climbs to her feet.)

NAUSICAA: Smack it / smack it / then /

(She dares him with her expression. TOT seems to weigh the proposal.)

You think Nausicaa juvenile / a schoolgirl who in her pink and pillowed bedroom pines for sickly men / their ribs bone cages to which cling bleeding songbirds / yes /

Nausicaa is condemned to love all liars / she asks one thing only / that they lie magnificently /

(She regards TOT boldly.)

The queen knows how poorly you would sing if / like Pindar / you got prizes / you know / do you not / the perverse pleasure she obtains from mocking him with her hyperbole? /

TOT: I wish she'd mock me similarly /

NAUSICAA: Yes / how could it be otherwise? / If you rejoiced in your condition you would be a liar of another kind / Tot /

(Now TOT slaps NAUSICAA, sending her sprawling. The relief he derives form this act is, however, curtailed when she suffers a fit as a consequence of his temper. She twitches. TOT's single fist clenches and unclenches.)

TOT: DOC – TOR /

(He calls aimlessly.)

DOC – TOR /

65

TOT's attention is so firmly fixed on NAUSICAA he is unaware of shadowy figures clustering about the perimeter of the stage. Only as NAUSICAA's fit diminishes does he sense their presence. At last she is still.

TOT: *(Sensing danger.)* Doctor / ha / what's that? / doctor / I haven't used that word since / God knows when / scum / filth / in their white coats / I DO KNOW WHEN / I DO KNOW WHEN / white coats / unbuttoned / flying like streamers in the wind / as if urgency condemned them to abolish buttons / as if / like angels' wings / the flapping of their overalls announced their merciful appearance / WHEN THIS ARM CAME OFF / THAT WAS WHEN /

DOCTOR I / what? / I / what was it I? / What was the
manner of my / can't remember / DOCTOR I / first word /
no / not the first / the first was / CHRIST / FUCK / JESUS /
any number of expletives / can't be precise / then / yes /
DOCTOR I BAWLED /

(He laughs, insincerely.)

A /

(TOT feels unsafe under the gaze of the encroaching figures.)

A /

(He squirms.)

Residual / invocation / triggered by shock /

(He feels compelled to justify himself further.)

Did I want a doctor? / EMPHATICALLY NOT /

(He is inspired by his own invention to invent further.)

Did I want the intensity of this experience to be
diminished? / Did I want some drab mechanic with his
toolbag / some flesh-fixer with an itching scrotum and
half-a-dozen words designed to terrify the terrified / did I
want his jargon and bad breath contaminating the terrible
meeting of Tot and his ally Death / I did say ally / yes / in
this instance he visited / and did not stop /

(He lifts his eyes to the figures.)

So doctor's / in my case / a curse /

(He shakes his head, as if renouncing hope.)

Don't send me back to prison /

66

To TOT's relief and amazement, the crowd of figures begins to laugh, spontaneously, and even to clap. TOT looks from one to another, and starts to laugh himself. NAUSICAA, as if she had never fallen, skips to her feet.

NAUSICAA: THE POET BRINGS US HEALTH / THE POET BRINGS US HEALTH /

(The crowd drifts off, turning and saluting TOT as they depart.)

BY DYING ALL THE TIME / BY DYING / AND COMING BACK AGAIN /

(She is momentarily ashamed of her enthusiasm.)

I think / when you do die / Tot / when Death pays you another visit / and for some reason impossible to guess / won't go without you / dragging your shirt / stamping his feet / a spoiled child is Death / I think / when that day comes / take me /

(TOT frowns.)

TOT: I don't desire you / Nausicaa /

NAUSICAA: No / and how perfect that is / since I don't desire you / we exist beyond desire / the singer / and the sung-to / it's a / oh / it's an intimacy / an intimacy which /

(NAUSICAA falters.)

Is impossible to explain /

TOT: Nausicaa feels no desire for the poet Tot / and the old Queen Eko / who says of song / it makes all pain possible / she profoundly admires him / but will not give him breakfast / or a kennel to keep the rain off him / I have to say / to be a poet / it's /

(He lifts his one hand.)

A /

(He creates a terrible smile.)

A /

NAUSICAA: It doesn't matter / your loveless poverty /

(He looks cruelly into NAUSICAA.)

TOT: I nearly said /

Ha /

I nearly said /

NAUSICAA: I know what you nearly said /

TOT: But I didn't /

NAUSICAA: You didn't / no /

TOT: I SO NEARLY SAID / PITIFUL /

NAUSICAA: Pitiful / yes /

TOT: IT MATTERS TO ME /

(He hangs his head.)

I nearly said it / the hesitation saying it / presumably / was caused by some / bottomless horror / that justice / and so on / is inapplicable to me /

(A terrible cry distracts TOT.)

67

TOT and NAUSICAA are frozen. Slowly, they turn their heads, as if to catch a sound on the wind. At last the cry comes again. Simultaneously, they recognize its origin.

NAUSICAA: In /

(She is agonized.)

In / in /

(The cry becomes a drawn-out sob.)

In / tensity /

TOT: And without medicine /

(NAUSICAA, as if summoned, hurries away. The public, individually and in groups, hastens over the stage, silent, earnest, their heads lowered, as if to a scene of grief or national mourning. A dense whispering rises. TOT, indecisive, goes to follow NAUSICAA. PINDAR, entering with a wealthily-clad QUASIDOC, calls him.)

68

PINDAR: NEW WORLD /

(The cry of EKO travels.)

A despot dies / and as she sinks / hope rises / as if her cries of agony beckoned to an era that had stood shivvering outside her door /

(He imitates a laugh.)

THIS WAY THE FUTURE / GRAB THE HANDLES AS IT RACES BY / TO THE NEW WORLD THIS TRAM / ONE WAY ONLY / DING / DING / MOVE DOWN INSIDE /

TOT: The despot was all right to you / as for the new / fuck the new / I never liked it /

(QUASIDOC laughs.)

PINDAR: Well / no / it won't suit Tot /

TOT: *(A rare moment of irony.)* You see how I have prospered /

(The cry of EKO.)

My extensive wardrobe / my vast estates / a change of government / I could lose the lot /

(QUASIDOC laughs again.)

PINDAR: I was thinking / from the stylistic point of view / how Tot's not qualified to serve the new / Tot can't sing praises /

QUASIDOC: Perhaps he's never wanted to? /

PINDAR: *(Stung.)* Perhaps he hasn't / and you don't need to lick him / does she / Tot? / Tot knows the new insists on new vocabularies / which he / it's honourable / of course / has not got / me neither /

(He grins.)

But over the grave / it's Pindar who will have to say / what? / Goodbye / presumably / but in such a way as to imply / despite the prizes / I despised the old bitch / lend us a phrase / Tot /

(He laughs, like a schoolboy.)

I'LL PAY /

(PINDAR laughs again, shaking his head.)

No sense of humour /

(Individuals and groups hurry by.)

Come along / the doctor-killer's pain might be relieved by the last doctor / the irony is / compelling /

(QUASIDOC is still. PINDAR senses her reluctance, and the cause of it.)

Surely? /

(QUASIDOC lifts her eyes to TOT.)

Irresistible / even? /

(QUASIDOC is resolutely still, her gaze falls. PINDAR is wounded, but conceals it. He seems to lend QUASIDOC time, then turns on his heel and walks smartly away in the same direction as the public. The cry of EKO floats over the scene.)

69

QUASIDOC lifts her eyes to TOT. She speaks in a way that serves to obscure the content, not inarticulate but fast.

QUASIDOC: The cock of a bad poet is no less hard and no less strong than the cock of a good poet still you long for the good poet's cock /

(TOT wonders if he has properly heard. Scattered individuals pass by. TOT's inquisitive look causes QUASIDOC to laugh like a mischievous schoolgirl.)

The cock of a bad poet is no less hard and no less strong than the cock of a good poet still you long for the good poet's cock /

(She bites her lip.)

My poem /

(She sniffs.)

Well / you pick it up / living with a poet / you pick up poetry /

(The cry of EKO.)

Say it's a poem /

(TOT declines to satisfy her, and his silence forces her on.)

If you had two arms I would not want you / funny /

(Again TOT makes no response.)

He doesn't sleep / Pindar / his heart / it gnaws / it doesn't beat / as if the ventricles were full of soldiers / would you like this fur coat? / have it / I'm naked underneath / NO I'M NOT /

(She laughs. The cry of EKO.)

I'm not / I'm not /

(TOT observes her.)

I don't know what it is / I'm not the only one / I'm not alone in liking one-armed men / when I worked in the hospitals / if you remember hospitals / they said / not said / said no / they pleaded / SEW MY ARM BACK ON AGAIN /

(EKO's cry.)

Idiots / I am / I am naked underneath /

(Still TOT tortures her by his silence.)

It's good / that silence / clever / clever altogether /

TOT: She brought back cries / birth / sickness / even love / because with all these sounds returning / sounds the doctors had smothered under chemistry / came a longing for the sound / the woman sound / in fucking / and madmen / oh / like wolves on frontiers / some nights / ha / frantic choruses / all right / I'll have you / my one hand in your belly / let the tits queue / swelling with anticipation /

(He roughly turns QUASIDOC, who exults.)

70

The dying EKO is hauled through the floor, but swiftly now, as the public rushes in, partially obscuring TOT / QUASIDOC's copulation, and crying out with pity or despair, the whole assembly acquiring the ecstatic quality identified by TOT and creating a dissonant music.

71

BLOK: *(Limping miserably on the perimeters.)* Can't watch / can't watch /

QUOTA: Darling / she says / oh / darling / where are you? /

BLOK: Can't watch /

QUOTA: *(Cradling EKO's head on her pillows.)* Then the Great Song of Death / she says / never will be written /

BLOK: By me / no /

(A cry from EKO startles BLOK.)

THE POET ALSO CAN DESERT HIS STATION /

(He suffers, his hands are fists of shame.)

I cannot witness this / I love you / and why I cannot / I do not know /

QUOTA: Go down to the garden / she says / place yourself under the window / hear what you hear / and when it's over / a handkerchief / wet with her tears / will fall / a sign / then climb the stairs again / and kiss her / if any man knows how to kiss / she says / it's you / this kiss she'll feel / though she will not be here / neither will she be gone /

(BLOK turns to leave.)

BLOK / BLOK /

(He stops.)

She says / she says /

(QUOTA frowns with the effort of interpretation.)

THIS IS THE ORIGIN OF THE SONG /

(QUOTA half-laughs for EKO. BLOK, troubled, turns, and encounters PINDAR by him.)

PINDAR: How infinitely / infinitely /

(He strains.)

INFINITELY /

(He shakes his head.)

Subtle / the old woman is /

(BLOK's mouth twitches.)

For forty years she's loved you / playing the empress /
playing the whore / impossible to measure your pleasures /
and now / for all that she loves you /

(He bites his lip in wonderment.)

For all that she needs you /

(BLOK hangs his head.)

SHE LOVES POETRY MORE /

(Suffused with shame, the old man goes to return to the bedside.)

QUOTA: GO / GO /

(BLOK stops, and after a slight hesitation obeys. He edges from the chamber of death. As he departs, EKO moans. PINDAR advances through the whispering crowd. He mutters to QUOTA.)

PINDAR: There is one doctor /

(EKO cries out.)

Did you hear me? /

(And again.)

Just one / one doctor / she's forgotten nothing / she can be
/ nobody needs to know / got in / and /

(EKO cries out.)

Pain-relief / it was a speciality of hers /

(QUASIDOC, in her ecstasy, cries out. PINDAR hears or senses this. He ceases his urging. He steps back. QUOTA, obedient to EKO's needs, hoists her up on her pillows. The old woman stares at PINDAR through pain-racked eyes.)

QUOTA: Hideous your pity / hideous / she says /

PINDAR: *(As if he were wounded.)* Pity / how can it be hideous?
/ It's pity /

(He looks in his bewilderment to NAUSICAA. EKO emits a terrible cry. BLOK, hearing it in the garden, seems to shrink with her pain.)

72

The white handkerchief floats like a leaf towards BLOK, who stares up at the window as instructed. It arrives, and settles over his head. He remains still, not attempting to remove it. Only his hands, moving agonized, describe his grief. The mourning of the public is like a deep pulse. Wilfully choosing not to remove the handkerchief, he feels his way, as if touching walls, back up the staircase.

73

As BLOK arrives in the death chamber, the public falls silent. His shoes creak in their usual way. With one hand before him, he senses his way to the bed. He pauses beside the body of EKO. The intensity of the silence owes much to the agony that preceded it. BLOK tilts, he lifts a hand, then snatches away the handkerchief. His eyes are tightly shut. He stirs, like a great tree in a gale. The public departs, discreetly.

74

BLOK: *(At last.)* I should not have lived this long /

PINDAR: Possibly /

BLOK: So many sights / so many odours / and these must be included /

PINDAR: Probably /

BLOK: Oh yes / these odours and these sights / are also poetry /

(He seems fixed. He turns his face towards PINDAR.)

Open my eyes for me /

(PINDAR is puzzled. He casts a glance at QUOTA, then at NAUSICAA.)

PINDAR: Open your /

BLOK: *(Who has intuited PINDAR's confusion.)* He thinks I am indulging myself with a metaphor / it's literal / uncrust my eyelids for me / please /

(For a moment, hesitation is universal. Then NAUSICAA, snatching a handkerchief from her sleeve, spits into it and going to the old man, attends to his needs.)

PINDAR: *(Pondering.)* I should do that /

(Then, vehemently.)

NAUSICAA / HE ASKED ME /

(She ignores him. PINDAR turns away. He frowns.)

How beautiful that might have been / if I / supreme among young poets / had with my own saliva / freed the gummed eyelids / of the last great singer / how entirely apposite / how / of all my life's contrivances / that / uncontrived / might have been legendary /

(He chokes bitter tears.)

Thank you for presenting me / dear man / with an opportunity I / in character / oh / so typically / thwarted / I loathe you / Nausicaa / OF COURSE I DON'T /

(He turns his back. His shoulders rise and fall in his misery. NAUSICAA holds BLOK by one hand, her handkerchief in the other. BLOK opens his eyes. He gazes on EKO's face.)

75

NAUSICAA frees the old man's hand, and withdraws, moving backwards over the stage.

76

QUASIDOC: Fuck me again /

TOT: *(Dubious about his ability to repeat the act.)*

I /

QUASIDOC: All right / something else /

(He hesitates.)

Another thing /

AM I BEAUTIFUL OR NOT? /

(TOT looks at her.)

Is that contempt? /

(He does not alter. QUASIDOC is volatile.)

IF THAT'S CONTEMPT /

TOT: I'm Tot /

(QUASIDOC frowns, insecure under TOT's regard.)

I'm Tot /

QUASIDOC: I heard you /

TOT: TOT /

QUASIDOC: Yes /

TOT: TOT /

QUASIDOC: All right / you're Tot /

TOT: *(Mechanically and terribly.)* TOT / TOT /

77

BLOK leans to the lips of EKO.

78

QUASIDOC strides swiftly to TOT and goes to smack him over the face. TOT employs his one hand to grasp her wrist.

TOT: TOT / TOT /

79

PINDAR turns to witness the kiss between BLOK and the dead queen. He involuntarily shakes his head in wonder.

80

TOT and QUASIDOC sustain a rigid stare.

TOT: TOT /

(With her free hand QUASIDOC slaps TOT over his cheek.)

81

QUASIDOC is overwhelmed by tears, PINDAR by song.

PINDAR: Number them / the kisses / number them / the eleven thousand and eight hundred kisses of a man condemned to kiss never again / and then / distinguish the perfect / separate the deep kiss from the shallow / leaving five hundred and / five hundred and /

(PINDAR seems to calculate the figures.)

Ninety-nine / we call divine / of which / just forty-two / caused him to / faint /

82

As PINDAR watches, the bed and the body descend through the floor, leaving BLOK poised. Similarly immobile, TOT and QUASIDOC gaze at one another. PINDAR breaks the stillness with a triumphant turn to the remaining observer of the death scene, QUOTA.

PINDAR: I see a thing / oh / isn't this the beauty of my method? / I see it / I see it and I suffer it / as if it were *my* ugliness / or *my* pain / and drawing this into my depths / as grit / presumably by error / is swallowed by the oyster / I make the painful /

(PINDAR's hands mould the air.)

EXQUISITE /

(He half-laughs with his triumph. QUASIDOC goes to pull away from TOT. He holds her.)

But quickly / I don't take years doing it / I am / ha /

(His eyes shine, intimidating QUOTA.)

THE FAST OYSTER /

(He seems to plead with her.)

Isn't that what makes me /

(He looks at her, smiling peculiarly, and vulnerable.)

THE POET OF THE AGE? /

(QUOTA feels herself transfixed by PINDAR's urgency. She contrives to nod her head. PINDAR advances on her. He now struggles to articulate his pain.)

Why don't you worship me? /

QUOTA: Worship you? /

PINDAR: *(Disarmingly simple.)* Worship me / yes /

(QUOTA tries to smile, a tactic to abolish tension. QUASIDOC goes to surge away from TOT, but can't. She stares. She slaps him again.)

I'm perfectly serious /

(She attempts to shrug her shoulders.)

To ask that question / not only of you / but of the world / but only you are here / so you must be the world / to frame the question / let alone to utter it / was not easy / yet / once I framed / and once I uttered it / it felt /

(He frowns.)

Probably the cleanest sentiment I ever expressed /

(QUOTA is relieved by his sincerity, but unable to speak.)

You should worship me / it is your tragedy that you cannot /

(Her eyes falter. PINDAR has no intention of relieving her discomfort, and continues to regard her. Swiftly, he turns and goes to leave. QUOTA calls.)

QUOTA: Mr Pindar /

(He stops. QUASIDOC tries to escape TOT, but he is dogged. She repeats the slap.)

One thing she said / one thing / forgive me / I failed to communicate /

(PINDAR anticipates, both in hope and dread.)

She wished you a life of painlessness /

(He absorbs her message. He moves on, but the stooping figure of BLOK compels his attention. He stops.)

PINDAR: What if we said / it hardly matters / since you are nearly / and I will be / at some time in the future / dead / what if we said /

(He sniffs, as if dismissing embarrassment.)

I cleaned your eyes? /

(BLOK makes no response, which encourages PINDAR.)

I am thinking / not of myself / but of mankind / how mankind lacks /

BLOK: Yes /

PINDAR: Yes? /

(They tacitly agree.)

AS IMAGERY GOES / OH / APOTHEOSIS OF / I SEE THIS AS THE INSPIRATION OF A CULTURE / A TESTAMENT TO KINDNESS / GREATER / YES / WHY NOT PROCLAIM IT? / GREATER THAN AENEAS BEARING ANCHISES ON HIS SHOULDERS / THE FLIGHT FROM TROY / HIS FATHER ON HIS BACK / AND IN ONE HAND / THE BOY / WAS THAT AUTHENTIC? / POSSIBLY / BUT IF IT WAS A POET'S SENTIMENT / WITH NO BASIS IN REALITY / DOES IT DETRACT? / WE MAKE TOO MUCH OF THIS / THIS / DUBIOUS VIRTUE / THIS EMPIRICAL EMPHASIS / SO THIS OCCURRED / SO THIS DID NOT / SO IT WAS HER HANDKERCHIEF / NOT HERS / THE WOMAN ON THE RIGHT OF HIM / NO / LEFT / RIGHT / RIGHT / ASSUREDLY / HER HANDKERCHIEF / BUT NOT / WE PROVE IT SCIENTIFICALLY / NOT HER SALIVA / OH / IT'S SILLY / SILLY / A PREJUDICE / A NAUSEATING ARCHAEOLOGY /

(He jeers.)

GET YOUR LITTLE HAMMERS OUT / AND YOUR RULERS / SIFT THE EVIDENCE / TAP / TAP / SIFT / SIFT /

(He laughs. He recovers. BLOK has not moved. PINDAR is embarrassed by his own enthusiasm.)

The point is this / Blok was blind with grief / the greatest poet of his day / he could not see / so Pindar stepped up to him / and wiped away the tears /

(He observes BLOK, stooping and fixed.)

Pindar / who with the passing of the years / wrote greater things /

(He is reluctant, playing with his fingers.)

That's necessary / or the scene's got no / no / resonance /

(He is at his most delicate.)

It places me under an awful obligation / obviously /

(BLOK is uninterested in PINDAR's speculations. PINDAR turns to go. He sees TOT and QUASIDOC, distantly. A tree descends, roots first.)

83

TOT has maintained his grip on QUASIDOC's wrist, in spite of her punctuating blows. She goes to repeat the action, but sensing its futility, lets her raised hand fall again.

QUASIDOC: So we are / we are something / what is it we are? / what / what / are we? / the thing we / something obviously / something now we were not previously / what / diagnostic / diagnostic me / one word / sufficient probably / one / to take away with me / so they are / him and her / something called / what / a word / Tot / it is so / you have the words / necessary to my /

(Suddenly she turns away. At once TOT releases her.)

So there's no word for it /

(She looks back at him.)

TOT: I thieve /

(He looks. He smiles, forlornly.)

What I have not stolen means nothing to me /

(QUASIDOC frowns.)

Blame the old queen / she knew praise kills the poet / so / to preserve / and not only to preserve / to intensify / his agony / she commanded him / live off the land / scrounge / thieve / be indigent and criminal / it injured her / I think / to see me / falling / and falling / through nets of ridicule and poverty / but she / oh / Eko's heart was hard / if life was to be / short / and doctorless / men needed song / great song / to relieve their misery / they sing / not Pindar / do they? / Let us speak frankly / at the death of children / it's Tot they sing / badly sometimes / but / they sing me /

(He half-laughs. BLOK is edging towards them.)

It would be / you know as well as I do / to my advantage to hang you from a branch / the final doctor / will bring back long life / won't she? / Poor life but long / I see you with a flock of students / pouring down the steps of the academy / and my songs forgotten / DON'T RUN /

(QUASIDOC senses the tree settle behind her.)

The police stripped medicine out the libraries / but you know physicians / never one house / two / three or more / boats / cottages / the authorities were tired out / prising up the floorboards / digging up the lawns / ten thousand volumes in the first year / it's fatiguing / obviously /

(TOT's expression is ambiguous.)

QUASIDOC: Knowledge is /

TOT: Shh /

(TOT lifts a hand to silence her. The place seems silent.)

QUASIDOC: Impossible to extinguish /

TOT: *(Irritably waving the hand.)* Shh / shh /

(He strains his hearing for a sound.)

QUASIDOC: Man loves knowledge / he /

TOT: *(Desperately.)* TSST /

(His face is a mask of strained concentration. QUASIDOC is reluctant, and purses her lips.)

84

The familiar sound of BLOK's creaking shoes precedes his appearance.

TOT: Here comes knowledge /

(TOT smiles with relief. His face is illuminated. His head tilted towards the direction of the sound, he is fixed in his ecstasy.)

You are shallow as a bowl / and all you do is ring / you should be drummed with a spoon / until you crack and chip / and the crack / expanding on a summer's night / should split / and all the shards go slithering / leaving your handle / swinging on the hook / you know nothing / of anything / of all things / you are ignorant / ping / you go / you go ping / ping /

(BLOK, his head low with his misery, edges on stage.)

Ping / this / pinging / pinging / the entire length of your flesh / ping / your portion on the earth / ping-ful / ping-packed / all ping you are / your ping-heart / your ping-head / ping-everything / your womb a ping-place / throbbing / throbbing your vulva with its stream of ping / I drink it / ping you taste / ping the odour / all things with you / the mouth / the words that leave it / crawling / soddened with the stuff of ping / the injury to hearing / ping you go / grinning / ping now / and ever ping /

(BLOK attains the tree and sinks at its foot.)

HE WALKED / IF YOU CAN CALL THAT WALKING / FROM ONE WORLD TO ANOTHER /

(He goes to BLOK, as if to comfort him, and fusses.)

Bits of the old world on his shoes / and on his waistcoat / stains of loyalties / only fit for ridicule / ping him / ping him /

(He turns brusquely to QUASIDOC.)

GOT A COMB THERE? / GOT A LITTLE LADY'S BRUSH? /

(QUASIDOC seethes, and is recalcitrant.)

His hair's / it's all / the wind / I can't / when someone looks like that / take heed of him /

(She is unyielding. TOT is near to violence.)

Please /

(He closes his eyes.)

PLEASE / MAKE THIS OLD MAN PROPER /

(QUASIDOC senses the danger to herself and strides over to the tree, removing a handbrush from her pocket.)

His hair is parted on the left /

(QUASIDOC, tightening her lips, proceeds to restore BLOK's appearance. TOT makes an irritated gesture to urge QUASIDOC to move away. She assents.)

85

PINDAR, idly, stands on the perimeter of the scene, watching TOT's fascination with BLOK, who is slumped, alive but barely. A low wind moans. A flock of birds passes, shrill but brief. TOT conducts his anticipation with his one hand. His back bends, and straightens like a sapling in a wind.

TOT: Knowledge / I said / here comes knowledge / ha /

(He is patient.)

He knows it all / and would he call it knowledge? / I don't think so /

(He stares at the old man. He walks up and down, stops.)

There is knowing / and there is after-knowing /

(He works his fingers together.)

SING IT / NOW / SING IT /

(He rebukes himself.)

I'm impatient / I'm impatient / as if I didn't know the pain of poetry / mind you / I know this too / you can give too much to a word / this word and not that one / the hands reach down / the swamp of the vocabulary / it's / sticky / deep / you fail to notice your feet / they're stuck / now you can't run / oh yes / we all know that phenomenon / poets must run / they're runners /

(He has a dread.)

SING IT / BLOK /

(BLOK is motionless.)

What is it? / cold / is it? / you're sitting in the sun /

(He looks to QUASIDOC.)

Give him your coat /

(QUASIDOC frowns.)

The leopard-skin / drape the old man with it /

(She is unwilling.)

So you are naked / be naked / naked and the last thing female seen by him / privileged the pair of you /

(QUASIDOC dithers. TOT menaces her.)

WHAT ARE YOU AFRAID OF? / THAT HE MIGHT VOMIT OVER IT? / SACRED IS THE OLD MAN'S BILE /

(QUASIDOC slips off the fur. TOT snatches it and goes to BLOK. He spreads it with some tenderness. QUASIDOC stands, at first uncomfortably.)

(To BLOK.) Warmer / eh? / so sing / sing /

86

PINDAR, his hands in his pockets, strolls nearer. Sensing him, QUASIDOC drops her hands and poses, defiantly.

PINDAR: *(With an eye on QUASIDOC.)* He did not watch her die / his ever-love / he fled /

TOT: *(Not removing his gaze from BLOK.)* He fled / did he? / Then let him sing his fleeing / and if he betrayed / betrayal is his song / the long / slow / rhythm of apology / I like it / young poets / let them sing joy / and the old ones / moan /

PINDAR: *(Strolling to the prostrate figure.)* HE WAITED IN THE GARDEN / TOT /

TOT: *(Rebuking PINDAR.)* IMMENSE THE OLD MAN'S CRIME / THEN /

(They stare at one another.)

And commensurate with that /

IMMENSE THE POEM HE GOT FROM IT /

(TOT lurches to BLOK.)

SING YOU / SING WHAT YOU DID / AND WHAT YOU FAILED TO DO /

87

BLOK's utter immobility enrages tot.

TOT: SING IT /

(Failing to elicit a response from the dying man, TOT resorts to kicking him.)

SING / SING /

PINDAR: *(Incredulous.)* You're kicking him /

TOT: IT'S THERE / THE POEM /

PINDAR: *(To QUASIDOC.)* HE'S KICKING HIM /

TOT: *(Raining kicks on BLOK.)* SING YOU / SING /

PINDAR: *(His hands crushed at his sides.)* STOP / TOT / STOP / STOP / STOP / TOT / PLEASE /

(Abandoning his attack on BLOK, TOT proceeds to drag the old man half-upright and shake him as a dog shakes a doll.)

TOT: IT'S THERE / IT'S THERE /

QUASIDOC: *(An appalling meditation.)* The poet kicks the poet /

PINDAR: TOT / TOT /

QUASIDOC: The poet brushes the poet's hair /

PINDAR: *(Weeping.)* TOT / HE'S DEAD / HE'S DEAD /

QUASIDOC: The poet dislocates the poet's shoulder /

PINDAR: DEAD / TOT /

TOT: WHO CARES? / WHO CARES? /

(With his single hand TOT grasps BLOK by his chin and glares into his empty eyes.)

The song / the song /

QUASIDOC: A cold child is the poet /

TOT: *(Acknowledging defeat.)* I could snap off this head / and like a bottle not quite empty / tip it up / and drain it for its dregs / a last half-glass before it's flung away / so with the old man's brain / there was half-a-poem in it / half / this half / more beautiful than anything he wrote /

(He looks at QUASIDOC.)

I say beautiful / what do you think? /

(QUASIDOC looks at TOT, half-provocative.)

Take the coat /

(She barely moves to his order.)

Thank you / he says / the perfume / the woman-sweat /
the woman sweat smothered in perfume / he was divinely
drowning / slaps / punches / nothing could call him out of
there / I should have known /

*(QUASIDOC walks to the body and discreetly bending, plucks up her
fur. She drapes it swiftly over her shoulders and leaves. PINDAR is
taut, pale, strained.)*

PINDAR: Not long ago / a poet wiped a poet's eyes / taking a
clean handkerchief / he moistened it with his own saliva
/ and tenderly / in order not to bruise the thin skin there
/ he soothed away the crust of grief that blinded him /
few things more moving in the history of the world / few
things? / Nothing / nothing more moving but /

(PINDAR is agonized.)

SOMETHING MORE / MORE /

(He appeals to TOT.)

WHAT IS MORE / WHAT IS / MORE BEAUTIFUL THAN PITY
/ TOT? /

(PINDAR cannot articulate a thought profoundly terrible to him.)

TOT: The song was there / but stuck in his gizzard / like a
fishbone / not a long song / you know Blok / four lines
at the most / choking possibly / but choking's policy / I
saw blokes choke in prison / on a single word / sorry / for
example /

PINDAR: EXQUISITE WAS YOUR VIOLENCE / TOT /

TOT: *(Looking at the ground.)* That was a song I needed / oh /
how I required that song /

(He shrugs.)

Still / the song was not my property / so /

(He smiles an ugly smile.)

Robbery with violence /

(TOT throws a desperate glance towards PINDAR.)

I CAN'T GO BACK TO PRISON /

PINDAR: *(With conviction.)* THE POET OWES THE PEOPLE NOT
ONLY HIS JOY / ALSO HIS SIN /

TOT: Does he? / I don't know /

PINDAR: I'm saying it was me /

TOT: What? /

PINDAR: Kicked Blok to death /

TOT: You? /

PINDAR: PINDAR KICKED THE OLD MAN / NOT FOR
HIMSELF / FOR POETRY /

Say that /

(PINDAR is feverish with excitement.)

AND STRESS HOW MERCILESS IT WAS / AN ATTACK OF
EXTRAORDINARY SAVAGERY /

(His mind vaults.)

I'll call her as a witness / whatever I say / she'll agree /
DON'T ARGUE / TOT /

TOT: I'm not /

PINDAR: TOT'S NOT / TOT'S NOT ARGUING / IS HE? /

*(PINDAR is half-hysterical, marching up and down. He stops,
abruptly.)*

88

NAUSICAA is discovered, holding a chair.

PINDAR: To destroy the master / because the master would not speak / because he would not share / but clung / like an infatuated infant to his creation / denying us when our souls flung themselves / pleading and howling / at his feet / to beat / to kill / a hail of fists and execration / far from barbaric is / is /

(PINDAR wrings his hands.)

THE PASSION OF THE PEOPLE /

(He is incandescent.)

DEMOCRACY IS ALSO RAGE /

(PINDAR seems content with his version of events. He observes NAUSICAA, who moves slowly downstage, her gaze on the body of BLOK.)

89

PINDAR: *(As NAUSICAA frowns.)* I kicked him / STOP SAID TOT / I couldn't stop / STOP / STOP / his one arm pulling mine like some scarecrow in a hospital / or on the bankside of the Styx as Charon brings his oar down on the skull of some reluctant tramp / STOP / OH / STOP /

(PINDAR smiles, kicks the ground idly.)

To let the old man sink into his grave / those final lines not spoken / I could not /

(NAUSICAA looks from BLOK to PINDAR, a look which causes PINDAR to seethe.)

You look in / in / incredulous /

(NAUSICAA looks from PINDAR to TOT. Distantly, public rejoicing. TOT is ashlar.)

What is the chair for? / To stand on for a better view? / Or to help you hang? / I have to say / Nausicaa / I don't see you in the new world /

(NAUSICAA regards PINDAR without opinion.)

The Doctrine of Intensity / who dares enunciate its principles today?

90

The public swarms in, euphoric. Transported on a door recently dragged off its hinges, QUASIDOC in a flying white medical coat. On another, students of medicine, also in medical garb, grinning and sheepish. All are carried shoulder-high. The public, in an ecstasy of relief, booms its convictions.

LAMP: We murder sickness / And unhappiness / we strangle it /

SHEET: OLD MOTHER / WALK AGAIN /

LAMP: Beloved is the nurse who shields with her white hand our aching eyes /

RUBBER: LEGLESS LITTLE BOY / RUN NOW /

LAMP: The wise doctor smiles / removing her spectacles / says /

SHEET: OLD MAN / WE GIVE YOU LAUGHTER /

LAMP: This can be done / and with the minimum of inconvenience /

SHEET: AND LUNGS MY SHRIVELLED CHILD /

LAMP: The shriek of the unalleviated /

RUBBER: GO HOME / ALL DONE /

LAMP: Will never pierce the night sky / nor the stink of wounds /

SHEET: THAT DIDN'T HURT / DID IT? /

LAMP: Make us retch in the rooms of poverty /

91

The mass of joy falls suddenly silent. The sound of lonely corridors, and drifting trolleys, metallic, colliding. No one moves.

QUASIDOC: I watched thick weeds enclose the mortuary / and encrusted lamps swing when ceilings shifted out the horizontal / tiles lifted / lagged piping sank like slaughtered animals in pools of blue or copper chemistry / I saw pages swim the air / blown from an unhinged window as seeds are spilled in burning summers / but this day was cold / they clung / they rasped on lifeless / sagging / cables / I clutched one / damp-stained and frayed / it showed the torso of a man / a flayed man / and every vein / and every artery / was named / in Latin / and in Latin also / in a scroll beneath / the legend CONTRA MORTEM PETIMUS SCIENTIAM /

(The sound of doors caught by draughts in ekoing corridors, and loose windows.)

Printed in 1685 / in Amsterdam /

(She seems to suffer a shuddering attack.)

THERE IS A HAND INSIDE MY CLOTHES / WHOEVER PUT THE HAND THERE KINDLY / UNDER MY CLOTHES / A HAND / STOP / HAND / OW /

(She pleads.)

INSIDE MY CLOTHES / A HAND / REMOVE IT / SOMEBODY /

(Suddenly she laughs.)

STOP / NOW / LISTEN / STOP I SAID / OW / NO / NO /

(She writhes as if attacked.)

92

The door-bearers are stone gargoyles as QUASIDOC degenerates physically and emotionally, their mouths hanging from incredulity.

QUASIDOC: No / you can't / you can't / you can't / no / CONTRA MORTEM / ow / PETIMUS SCIENTIAM /

(She struggles.)

It's in my heart / it's got its fingers in / ow /

(She shrieks.)

SOMEONE'S HAND IS IN MY HEART /

(She falls onto her side on the door.)

The hospital is bigger than you / the mass / the volume / the sheer weight of the hospital / CONTRA MORTEM / ow / PETIMUS / ow /

(She grapples with her enemy.)

The intensification and / perpetuation of / the hospital / DO NOT QUARREL WITH THE HOSPITAL / OW / MY HEART / MY HEART IS /

(She is suddenly mild.)

Listen / my heart is being handled /

(She sits up abruptly.)

AND WITHOUT GLOVES /

(She lifts her hands, gazing down at her body.)

Listen / the ungloved hand / it pumps my blood for me /

93

QUASIDOC is radiant.

QUASIDOC: ALL THINGS WILL BE SEEN / AND ALL THINGS
ENTERED / WE SHALL WALK IN ONE ANOTHER / AND SIT
IN ONE ANOTHER / THE OPEN BODY / PLEASE / STROLL
THROUGH ME / AND WHERE I AM FLUID / ROW / ROW
IN ME / THE DOOR / YOU TRANSPORT ME ON A DOOR
/ HOW PERFECT YOUR DECISION / TO TEAR IT OFF ITS
HINGES / AN ACT WHICH SEEMED THE ESSENCE OF
SPONTANEITY / BUT NO / WE ABOLISH DOORS / LISTEN
/ OH / LISTEN / THE ATLAS OF ANATOMY / SHOWED ME
MAN ALSO COULD BE OPENED / FLUNG BACK HIS FLESH
/ THE BLAZING SUN REFLECTED IN HIS LIVER / AND
ON HIS LUNGS BREEZES AND POLLENS / NO INSIDE /
NO OUTSIDE / I WALTZ IN YOU / YOU JIVE IN ME / AND
SHOULD YOU SLIP IN MY EFFLUENTS / GRAB MY RIB /
SNATCH MY ARTERY /

(The public is infatuated with QUASIDOC's manifesto and laughing, hoists her higher. The students, inspired with the dignity of their profession, chant the Latin slogan as the crowd bears them away.)

94

The passage of the public leaves TOT and PINDAR revealed with spades in their hands, and NAUSICAA seated on the chair. They are uniformly dejected. PINDAR lifts his spade and thrusts it into the ground.

PINDAR: I should have strangled her / I didn't lack for
opportunities /

TOT: *(Lifting his spade with his single arm.)* Strangle her now /

PINDAR: I should do /

TOT: Do it / then / what's stopping you? /

(He thrusts in the spade.)

PINDAR: *(Observing TOT, who loosens earth.)* 'What's stopping me?' / 'What's stopping me?' / I could be sick hearing you / Tot / vilely sick / and this sickness originates not in the casualness with which you articulate the commonplace and sordid notions/ like murder / like torture / that occur to you / but in the fact / the indigestible and incongruous / and frankly / nauseating fact / you are able to create the most beautiful and /

(He shakes his head.)

I could cry / as a matter of fact / I am / I think / crying / beautiful and excoriating things / whilst /

TOT: *(Plunging in his spade again.)* Don't strangle her then /

PINDAR: *(Throwing down his spade.)* IT IS NOT THE VIOLENCE / TOT / THAT CAUSES ME TO SHUDDER /

(He glares at TOT, who regards him.)

How it serves you / in your appalling complacency / to consign me to the shuffling ranks of the tender and the squeamish / but it won't do / it will not do / because I have rage in me / more rage perhaps / than you / and know the sacred character of killing / believe me / when killing is / as it were / a /

(He struggles with the notion.)

A SEALED ENVELOPE / delivered / at the end of terrible contemplation /

TOT: There you are / then / do it /

(For a moment, PINDAR sways on his feet, his eyes closed. NAUSICAA, sensing the depth of his despair, rises to her feet, gazing on him.)

Imagine / will you? / I have brained you with the spade / I am no longer holding? / It is certainly what I wish to do / but having flung it down / I could not both retrieve it / and strike you /

(He shrugs.)

Small things like that / I try to describe in my / my most personal poems / 'Sonnet on the Late Arrival of a Longed for Visitor' / for example /

TOT: *(Gazing at PINDAR.)* I like that one /

(PINDAR dreads TOT's sarcasm.)

PINDAR: How could you like it? / It was never published /

(NAUSICAA is drawn to PINDAR, who shakes his head pitifully. She caresses him. TOT drives in his spade. He aches.)

TOT: It can't be done / burying Blok / I've got one arm / and you / you prefer to demonstrate how your heart hurts when someone says kick / fist / or bitch / no / let's sprinkle him / delicious say the foxes / poet tongue / poet lip / the cubs scrapping for fingers that once pressed the cervix of a queen as if it were a doorbell / admit me / am I not thin? / And young? / And pale with fear? / Blok knew more of dread than any man / his skin / if you breathed a harsh word / trembled like a lake in winter / I said no speeches / a few / a few /

(He flings earth over BLOK's body.)

Spadefuls /

(And another.)

Only a few / was that a speech? /

(He throws aside his spade.)

95

A pair of men in white coats hurry over the stage propelling a lolling patient in a wheelchair. He emits short groans. Tubes, bottles, half-detached, drag in the mud.

PINDAR: *(Removing himself from NAUSICAA's embrace.)* It is / I think / time we talked of mercy /

(A nimble cripple vaults over the stage on crutches, following the wheelchair.)

Not to others / but to ourselves /

(A distraught mother hurries in the same direction as the cripple, bearing a bawling child in a blanket. PINDAR lets her pass before drifting downstage.)

To eradicate from our vocabulary / certain words / that would be a start / for example /

(A senile couple, staggering and hurrying, collide with PINDAR as he wanders in his meditation.)

DON'T TOUCH ME /

(He flings the old woman away.)

A simple word I would submit might well be abolished is / sorry /

(The senile couple limp on.)

Obliterate the word / and other words / chained like galley-slaves to sorry / and all rowing in the same melancholy direction / are simultaneously demolished / admit / confess / apology / to some degree /

(He corrects himself.)

TO A CONSIDERABLE DEGREE / I confess /

(He lifts his hands in a sort of ecstasy.)

YOU SEE / I SAID IT / I SAID CONFESS / IT COMES NATURALLY TO ME / MY MOUTH IS LIKE HIGH TIDE IN A STORM-LASHED HARBOUR / AWASH WITH THIS / THIS /

(He gesticulates. a trio of sick individuals, one either side of a legless man, swing over the stage.)

FLOTSAM OF DEAD LANGUAGE / I was about to say / say / say simply / actually say / much of my work / was / informed by / if not permeated / soddened / dripping with

/ this poisonous and corrupting attitude of self-abnegation /
and I say attitude / it was / precisely / attitude / and whilst
it earned me /

*(A pair of whimpering old women collide with PINDAR as he surges
about the stage.)*

GET OUT OF MY WAY / GET OUT OF MY WAY / YOU
SMELL / YOU HORRIFY ME WITH YOUR DECAY /

*(The old women shriek as PINDAR raises a fist to them, and lurch
away.)*

Earned me / substantial recognition / I am now ready
and / more than ready / I rejoice to say / THOSE WORKS
WERE /

*(One of the old women sinks to the ground. PINDAR is aware of
it, and ceases in mid-flow. He himself looks stricken, and walks
falteringly towards them. The surviving old woman edges away in
fear of PINDAR, half-stooping, abandoning her companion. PINDAR's
body describes his pain.)*

96

*TOT walks slowly towards the group, holding the chair. He places it
behind the surviving old woman, and firmly presses on her shoulder,
compelling her to sit.*

SISTER: My sister /

TOT: Your sister /

SISTER: My sister / she was only 85 /

TOT: It's cruel / when beauty meets a murderer /

SISTER: Beauty? / I don't know that she was /

*(TOT stops the old woman's speech with a kiss, drawing her face to
his own with his single arm. The kiss is long and deep. TOT draws
her off the chair. They sink to the ground alongside the dead woman.
NAUSICAA, who has observed everything, puts a finger to her mouth,*

studious. PINDAR is fixed in wonder, shaking his head mildly from side to side.)

PINDAR: Oh / Tot / oh / always in his day / is Tot / in his day / and of his day /

(The old woman's legs rise, her skirts deftly plucked away by her lover.)

97

NAUSICAA occupies the chair. She observes the spectacle, her chin in her hand.

NAUSICAA: Odysseus / I said / It's impossible / it is simply / impossible / you are going away /

(The old woman cries out in her ecstasy.)

He looked / oh / dishonest / he looked / *himself* / to put it another way / which disappointed me / it is / surely / not too much to ask of a liar that he lies without displaying the many signs of lying / Odysseus shifted / literally / from foot to foot / did he always lie this badly? / Or was it my /

(The old woman cries out again.)

I don't hesitate to describe it / my / WITHERING SINCERITY / that in / in / induced in him this / EMBARRASSING EMBARRASSMENT? / Yes / his discomfort communicated itself to me / his shame / like some family of loathsome rodents / deserted him / and lodged in me /

(TOT rises to his feet. He looks down at the curiously still form of the old woman. He flicks her poor skirts over her nakedness.)

I thought / Odysseus is an education / but whether I am obliged to submit / and be altered by it / or to repudiate it / and remain / devoutly innocent / as I was when I set eyes on him / is / a decision /

PINDAR: *(Grimacing.)* KILLER /

NAUSICAA: For me /

PINDAR: *(Ecstatic.)* KILLER /

NAUSICAA: And only me /

TOT: *(Shrugging his shoulders.)* She /

PINDAR: THRICE /

TOT: She /

PINDAR: OH / THRICE / EVEN WHEN /

   (He laughs grotesquely.)

   WHAT HE INTENDS IS KIND / STILL HE KILLS /

TOT: You /

PINDAR: ME TOO / ME TOO / TOT / I KILLED ONE SISTER / BUT WITH / OH / BANAL BRUTALITY / WHEREAS YOU /

   (PINDAR dances with a surfeit of energy.)

   YOU / AND HERE I / OH / TOT / TOT / I YIELD THIS IMPERISHABLE STATUS TO YOU / MAKE DEATH YOUR VALET / LOOK HOW HE STANDS / AT A RESPECTFUL DISTANCE /

   (He is adoring, and still.)

   Is it surprising the old queen loved you? / When she howled on her death-bed / Tot / I think she howled for you /

   (He exults.)

NAUSICAA: I said no /

98

From the highest branches of the tree a rope-ladder spins and at its full length, idles in the air.

NAUSICAA: I said no / and heard no /

(PINDAR, his attention drawn by the rope ladder, drifts towards it.)

I heard my no / and thought it beautiful / and not knowing how no shapes the lips / the jaw and so on / I went to my mirror / to see no said / and it confirmed me in my opinion / how in its contours and its tone / no stops time and insolence / Nausicaa chose to let the world change / but to remain unchanged herself / a death-sentence / it goes without saying /

(She stands, and lifting the chair in one hand.)

E / DUCO / says the educator / 'let me lead you out of yourself' / but was Nausicaa not already perfect? / Was she to leave her innocence / like some discarded garment / on the beach? / I watched Odysseus go / and with his sinking sails / his education /

(She is scornful.)

E / DUCO /

(The feet of a man are discernible on the highest rung of the ladder.)

I was certain / and more than certain / determined / if Odysseus sailed in again / more stooping still with lying / again I would not deny him /

(The feet descend another rung.)

But go / white with credulity / white-armed Nausicaa / and her heart / white /

(She goes to move towards the tree.)

TOT: HOLD IT / HOLD IT / HOLD IT / HOLD WHAT? / HOLD ANYTHING / DARLING /

(TOT's warning stops her.)

Hold it / I like hold it /

(He shakes his head ruefully.)

I mean / delay your move towards /

(The feet descend, agonizingly. All three stare as the figure arrives at the lowest rung. It is too far off the ground to enable him to step onto the ground. The rope ladder sways a little, as if in a breeze.)

Whoever /

NAUSICAA: *(Going to assist the stranger.)* He can't /

TOT: *(Seizing NAUSICAA by her shoulder.)* HE CAN'T / NO / HE CAN'T / HE CAN'T / NO / SO /

(TOT releases NAUSICAA and precedes her, cautiously. He stops.)

Should he? /

(NAUSICAA frowns.)

Should he? / Should he? / Just because he can't / should he? /

(NAUSICAA is impatient, and goes to pass TOT. TOT grabs her.)

IT DOESN'T FOLLOW /

(He fixes her in his arm. All four figures are still.)

PINDAR: IT'S ODYSSEUS /

(TOT scoffs.)

Could be / could be /

TOT: *(Deriding PINDAR's proposition.)* Those long days of retirement / Ithaca / oh / dull / arid / less precious than he imagined it to be / goatskins on the marriage bed / and the body of Penelope / collapsed / and with a tendency to cry ouch when he spreads her knees / ouch / ouch / it's arthritis / and him / scarcely better / it takes it out of you / doing the Odyssey /

NAUSICAA: He's eighty-six /

TOT: Eighty-six / you see / she knows / and every birthday / makes a garland /

NAUSICAA: Yes /

TOT: A garland for a liar /

NAUSICAA: Yes /

TOT: PURE IS NAUSICAA /

(NAUSICAA evades TOT's grip and swiftly goes to the tree.)

DON'T HELP HIM /

(NAUSICAA stops, turns to TOT.)

If you place the chair beneath the ladder / the geezer on the ladder will step on the chair /

(She is resolute.)

Once he's on the chair /

(PINDAR laughs.)

Yes / yes /

(PINDAR advertizes his laugh.)

It's funny / it's funny / Pindar and me / we don't have much in common / but /

(NAUSICAA goes to arrange the chair. TOT's cry is terrible, long, unfamiliar.)

NAU – SIC – AA /

(She freezes. The ladder sways.)

You have to choose / darling / between poetry and innocence /

PINDAR: How's that / Tot? /

TOT: If she helps him off the ladder / it will be the death of me /

NAUSICAA: *(Bitterly.)* THAT ISN'T FAIR / IT ISN'T FAIR TO MAKE ME /

(She is speechless. She shudders. She recovers.)

I got this chair this morning / and walked with it / I carried this chair miles / you saw me /

PINDAR: What's she doing with that chair / I said /

NAUSICAA: I felt foolish / and it's awkward / you know how I hate it / when for any reason whatsoever / attention is drawn to me / the train was crowded / people were bruised / their shins / they cursed me / I apologized / and what was so / what made it particularly / painful / was the absurdity / I never / ever / do things that are absurd / or offend others / it made no sense to be / transporting this / this / it made no sense until /

PINDAR: The dimensions of the chair /

NAUSICAA: This / this /

PINDAR: Exactly correspond /

NAUSICAA: Ladder / dropped down / and he /

PINDAR: *(Tilting his head to view.)* To the gap between the last rung and /

TOT: *(Calm now.)* It's not Odysseus /

PINDAR: For want of a better word / the world /

TOT: It's not him /

NAUSICAA: It's in / in / insignificant / Tot / who it is / it might be Odysseus / it might not / the fact is / I woke with this /

TOT: Yes /

NAUSICAA: This /

TOT: Yes /

NAUSICAA: Obligation / or /

TOT: Yes /

NAUSICAA: IN / IN / INVITATION / I don't know what /

TOT: NAUSICAA / ALL RIGHT / PLACE THE CHAIR / PLACE IT / THE CHAIR / THE CHAIR / PLACE THE THING / THE CHAIR / ALL RIGHT / I / ONLY HUMAN / ME / AND HUMANS DIE / OLD WOMAN THERE / MY LAST LOVE / NEVER KNEW HER NAME / NO REASON WHY TOT SHOULD SURVIVE INTO THE AGE OF EVERLASTING / NO / NO / STICK IT THERE / THERE / THERE /

(He indicates the place. He is suffused in bitterness and sentimentality.)

Mother / in the demolished kitchen / steam and low voltage / starched shirts / boiled rice / why do you cook it / when you know I hate it? / The windows weep with condensation / wipe the windows / I can't stand the sight of weeping windows / as if night scared the glass / as if the frightened kitchen wept / I saw the pants of Miss today / by lying on the floor in games / the smell of boards / the smell of tweed as she / I tore a picture out of Greeks / as she / did you know Greeks wore skirts / warriors / short skirts / as she passed she / the red light on the cooker / the red light on the cooker is my best friend / my best friend / we /

(NAUSICAA arrives beneath the ladder. She sets the chair.)

99

For some moments the figure on the ladder makes no attempt to step down. PINDAR is if anything more tortured by anticipation than TOT, his hand rising, his fingers yearning. A pair of doctors race by, oblivious to the scene, their coats and stethoscopes flying. As if to break the tension, PINDAR marches forward to the tree, and extending a hand to the stranger, assists him in his descent. The man steps onto the chair then onto the ground, and as if at the end of his strength, sits heavily on the chair. Offstage laughter precedes the appearance of two electric wheelchairs. The occupants giggle at some anecdote. They pass over the stage. Silence returns.

100

PINDAR: *(Unable to tolerate further silence.)* Tot here is a savage poet / his subject matter / it's /

BRADY: I know Tot /

(PINDAR inclines his head.)

PINDAR: Crude occasionally / whereas me / perhaps to my own detriment / never renege on the contract I made with myself / at a very early age /

BRADY: Shut up /

PINDAR: At sixteen / with another now distinguished writer of works for the theatre / to first and foremost / be /

BRADY: Shut up /

PINDAR: Responsible to others / to articulate what / possibly / they lacked the / education or /

(BRADY lifts his eyes to PINDAR. PINDAR's gaze falls.)

I do not have to shut up /

(He is uncomfortable.)

I do not have to /

(BRADY is uninterested in PINDAR.)

TOT: Blok's gone /

BRADY: I saw /

TOT: Which makes it / somehow / less terrible for me /

BRADY: Does it? /

(Suddenly NAUSICAA collapses into a fit of weeping. The two electric wheelchairs traverse the stage in the opposite direction to their previous appearance, the occupants still voluble. NAUSICAA draws deep breaths.)

TOT: Oh yes / oh yes / less terrible / certainly / the world without Blok / already it was beginning to seem /

(His gaze meets BRADY's.)

Uninhabitable /

101

BRADY seems to measure TOT's worth.

BRADY: I brought the gun /

TOT: Thank you /

BRADY: Someone wants it / so don't be /

TOT: No /

BRADY: Too long about it /

TOT: No /

BRADY: Dismantling it /

TOT: Yes /

BRADY: And cleaning it /

TOT: Yes /

BRADY: Takes time / and I am / you know /

TOT: A perfectionist /

BRADY: I like to do things properly /

TOT: Ten minutes /

(BRADY is unimpressed.)

I say ten / why ten? / Why not five? / It's habit /
ten minutes we say / 'ten minutes I'll be away' / or /
conversely / 'I shan't stay more than ten minutes' / the
little lies of daily life / 'undress / undress' / 'I can't' / 'you
can' / 'my husband he's' / 'ten minutes / darling / only ten
minutes of your nakedness / I beg / I pray' / the sun sinks
on ten minutes / you're right to be suspicious / Brady /

(He indicates NAUSICAA and PINDAR.)

And they might /

(He waves a hand dismissively in the air.)

Delay me /

(He looks at them, smiling weakly.)

With love / and suchlike / considerations /

(He lets his hand and his head fall. He is still for a moment, and then launches himself decisively towards BRADY.)

Give us it /

(He goes close to BRADY, so the transaction is barely visible. PINDAR is inspired.)

PINDAR: HE'S /

(He heaves, as if with sickness.)

HE'S /

NAUSICAA: Tot /

(A group of wheelchairs passes over the stage, as if on a seaside promenade. Mild, dim conversation intermittent.)

PINDAR: HE'S /

NAUSICAA: Tot / Tot /

(TOT lurches away from BRADY, pulling at the mechanism.)

TOT: Good-bye /

PINDAR: NOT GOING TO /

> *(TOT has thrust the barrel of the gun to his chest.)*

> NAUSICAA /

NAUSICAA: *(At her most commanding.)* TOT /

PINDAR: ARE YOU? / YOU ARE NOT /

> *(TOT chooses not to pull the trigger at once. He looks at PINDAR.)*

TOT: You say I'm not / precisely to induce me /

NAUSICAA: Tot /

TOT: I could not go / I could not do / what this is / and leave him thinking / he was the cause of it / as if Pindar dared Tot / and Tot / proud as a schoolboy /

BRADY: Good point /

TOT: Shot himself out of bravado / no /

BRADY: Good point / it needed clearing up /

> *(TOT pulls the trigger. The sound of the shot expands, mixing and transforming into a pure note which runs beneath TOT's adieu. The occupants of the wheelchairs stare.)*

102

TOT: Immense / piano / dust / in sun / falling / dust falling / biscuit / cracked / the lino / scrubbed / boots / hand / old hand / so old / the hand / dropped it / the domino / floor / cat / dirt / wound / scab / five / immensely old / dip it / dip / the biscuit / dip the biscuit in the tea / five / dots / five / apron / flowers / stable / Joe / bites never / five dots / the domino / kicks never / Joe / nice loaf / kind animal / a nice loaf / please / say please / nice / loaf / crust / mother / apron / red light / red light / piano / did she / girl / mother / piano / horse / the maiden's prayer / apron / apron /

(TOT is dead.)

BRADY: Fetch it / darling /

(NAUSICAA is gazing on TOT's body.)

Gun / darling / fetch it / please /

(She seems not to hear.)

IT'S BOOKED / THE GUN / IT'S BOOKED FOR HALF PAST
THREE /

*(PINDAR goes to retrieve the weapon. He lifts it with a visible distaste
and delivers it to BRADY. His tone is replete with sarcasm.)*

PINDAR: The hire fee / I'll gladly settle it / I imagine you don't
give receipts? /

BRADY: *(Taking the gun.)* It's on the house /

(He wraps the weapon in a handkerchief.)

I never saw Tot charged for anything / breakfasts / whores
/ electricity / they ran cables off his neighbours / and the
neighbours / if they discovered it /

PINDAR: *(Bitterly.)* IT MUST BE PAID FOR / POETRY /

BRADY: They /

PINDAR: IT'S NOT RAIN / IT'S NOT SNOW / IS IT? /

BRADY: Were obliging /

PINDAR: IT DOESN'T FALL FROM THE SKY /

(PINDAR laughs, falsely. BRADY, stiff-jointed, rises from the chair.)

BRADY: Personally / I never understood it / Tot's poetry /

PINDAR: Did anyone? /

BRADY: I thought / I thought /

(BRADY seems troubled.)

I thought /

PINDAR: What? / What did a man think / who / if he didn't kill / helped killers kill? /

BRADY: There goes a brain /

(PINDAR affects bewilderment.)

PINDAR: There goes a brain? /

(BRADY limps away.)

THERE GOES A BRAIN? /

(BRADY ignores PINDAR, who is incensed.)

AND THAT / PITIFUL / IDLE /

(He grasps the air in his frustration.)

SENTIMENTAL / DEFERENTIAL / I nearly described it as an attitude / no / never an attitude / an attitude / to qualify as such / requires a thought /

(PINDAR shudders.)

'THERE GOES A BRAIN ' IS NOT A THOUGHT /

103

The curious occupants of the wheelchairs have been joined by surgeons and nurses. They advance, discreetly but decisively, on PINDAR and NAUSICAA. One of the surgeons kneels to TOT's body.

NAUSICAA: Heart in ribbons / he rehearsed it / with a toy / that shot / I said / they blow their heads off / normally / the suicides / he said my brain's a palace / a thousand rooms of treasure / I will not desecrate it / what do you think I am? / A yob? / An anarchist who wants to strut in a killed queen's underwear? / Spare me / spare me / his heart he cared for also / and to keep them both he might have hanged himself / an unspoiled body / bar the arm / but no / he guessed you'd lever out his heart / and stick it in another chest / Pindar's / for example /

PINDAR: I don't require a heart /

NAUSICAA: Another Pindar / so like Pindar /

PINDAR: No one is like me /

NAUSICAA: As to make no difference / Tot's soul would never rest /

PALLID: The liver / possibly /

NAUSICAA: It's rotten /

PALLID: Is it? / But the lungs / the lungs / they /

NAUSICAA: A mess / the lungs / encrusted / some days Tot could hardly breathe /

(The surgeon senses NAUSICAA's hostility.)

PALLID: The bones / the marrow in the bones / we /

NAUSICAA: Riddled / the bones /

PALLID: Is that so? /

NAUSICAA: Riddled / thoroughly /

PALLID: Riddled /

NAUSICAA: A rare disease from childhood / on top of that / arthritis /

PALLID: *(Standing.)* It's rare we cannot salvage something from a suicide /

NAUSICAA: He was in / in /

(She closes her eyes, tightens her fists.)

Incorrigibly selfish / I said someone might need those lungs / they way you go on / as if they were your own / they were lent to you / like borrowing from the library / you give the books back when they're finished / they're on loan /

(She glares at PALLID.)

In / in / incorrigible /

PALLID: *(Measuring NAUSICAA critically.)* Think of a dad /

(NAUSICAA frowns.)

A so-loved / oh / a so-loved dad /

(NAUSICAA is patient.)

Think of his daughter / at school / a pretty child / but always sad / why? / Because her dad is dying / painfully / and they both know she will / unlike her class / go through her tender years / without his kind hand on her shoulder /

(He looks deeply into NAUSICAA.)

I cannot understand why you /

NAUSICAA: IT'S GRIEVING /

(They gaze at each other in profound hostility, a contest ended when PALLID puts his fingers to his lips and whistles. Two men appear on the edge of the stage, carrying a stretcher and attend on a signal given by PALLID. NAUSICAA is defiant. PALLID looks away and clicks his fingers. The stretcher-bearers hurry over.)

Sing Tot / say /

(The men look at NAUSICAA. PALLID indicates they should lift TOT's body onto the stretcher.)

SING TOT TO SAD GIRLS /

(NAUSICAA shakes her head and weeps. As they carry the body off, she goes to rush after them but falls and lies stiff and motionless on the ground. The medical salvage team goes off, indifferent. The wheelchaired observers continue on their way.)

104

PINDAR, observing, delays going to NAUSICAA. When he senses they are alone, he moves to her, and stands close. He procrastinates.

PINDAR: I should have /

(He aches.)

I should have /

(He shakes his head.)

Joined Tot /

(He seems to sicken.)

I had the gun / when the gunman said / fetch it for me / instead of running to him like some sportsman's dog / I should have turned it on myself / a terrible and legendary repetition / one master of singing perishes / and then / it's scarcely credible / as if they hung on either side of poetry / strung up like game / the other one repeats the action / the second greater than the first because unmeditated / as if spontaneity burst through that endless measuring and discerning which is the curse of life /

(He purses his lips.)

But unlike Tot / I never rehearsed my suicide / and being Pindar / would have failed / and maimed / instead of murdering myself /

(As always, NAUSICAA scrambles swiftly to her feet.)

Eye hanging out / shattered jaw / comic ineptitude /

(He half-smiles.)

Of course / with all these surgeons / the mess would be restored /

NAUSICAA: Blok's heart fed fox cubs / Tot / he /

(She cannot elucidate the thought which follows.)

PINDAR: More than restored / enhanced /

NAUSICAA: Blok's brain / the rain washed into chalk / Tot / he /

(Again she is stopped.)

PINDAR: Nobody need negotiate some bitter truce with his own face / you find your nose offensive? / Study the catalogue /

NAUSICAA: Tot / he /

PINDAR: Select /

NAUSICAA: IS RENDERED /

PINDAR: A suitable replacement / yes he is / Nausicaa /

(She stares at PINDAR, ghastly.)

Like a calf / like a salmon / like a ewe / like a pig /

(She is fixed by PINDAR's icy recital.)

Like a hen / like an eel / like a hare / like a horse /

(He seems to writhe inside his own body.)

YOU ARE NOT MORE DISGUSTED THAN ME / NAUSICAA / NO ONE IS / OR EVER WILL BE / MORE HORRIFIED THAN PINDAR / HE SHUDDERS AS HE BREATHES /

(He is still.)

He runs through the rooms of himself / he screams / he collides with furniture / immense this furniture / if I am not a singer / still I say / there was nothing else I might have been /

(PINDAR is tight-lipped, to abolish weeping. NAUSICAA is susceptible. She frowns.)

NAUSICAA: Never be honest / Pindar / never be / for some it's /

(She searches for the word.)

Inappropriate /

(She makes a face.)

HOW HARD THAT IS / HOW HARD / TO HAVE TO BE / FOREVER / SCARCELY TRUTHFUL /

(PINDAR is wounded. he gazes at the ground.)

Carry me / Pindar /

(He looks at her, ashamed as a boy.)

Lift and carry me /

(With the slightest hesitation, PINDAR goes to NAUSICAA and picks her up in his arms. They are still. The world passes by them.)

Pindar / I do not want to tread the earth again / ever / ever /

(PINDAR senses the length and breadth of his burden.)

Say I need not / say the filthy ground / thick with crime and chemical / will never slop over Nausicaa's feet / like sewage spews out of a drain / when you are tired / fling me / as frantic parents chuck an infant on a cot / cursing / slamming doors / trembling to know how near they got to murder / or / if you prefer it / hang me / I shan't complain / but say it / say I need never / never / say /

(PINDAR finds the resources in himself to negate his own existence.)

PINDAR: Never /

Never /

Never /

(A knot of aged party-goers trails over the stage, laughing.)

Never /

Never /

*

Other Howard Barker titles from Oberon Books include:

Plays One
Victory · The Europeans · The Possibilities ·
Scenes from an Execution
£14.99 · 9781840026122

Plays Two
The Castle · Gertrude – The Cry · Animals in Paradise ·
13 Objects
£14.99 · 9781840026481

Plays Three
Claw · Ursula · He Stumbled · The Love of a Good Man
£14.99 · 9781840026764

Plays Four
I Saw Myself · The Dying of Today · Found in the Ground ·
The Road, The House, The Road
£14.99 · 9781840028515

Plays Five
The Last Supper · Seven Lears · Hated Nightfall
· Wounds to the Face
£14.99 · 9781840028867

Plays Six
(Uncle) Vanya · A House of Correction · Let Me ·
Judith · Lot And His God
£14.99 · 9781840029611

Dead Hands
£7.99 · 9781840024647

The Fence in its Thousandth Year
£7.99 · 9781840025712

The Seduction of Almighty God
£8.99 · 9781840027112

Slowly / Hurts Given and Received
£8.99 · 9781849430166

A Style and Its Origins
Howard Barker and Eduardo Houth
£10.00 · 9781840027181

Theatre of Catastrophe
New Essays on Howard Barker
£14.99 · 9781840026726

To order any of the above books, please contact:
Marston Books, PO Box 269, Abingdon, Oxon, OX14 4YN
Email: direct.orders@marston.co.uk
Telephone: 01234 465577, Fax: 01235 465556
Or visit

www.oberonbooks.com